THE BEST DEVOTIONS OF

Marilyn Meberg

GRAND RAPIDS, MICHIGAN 49530

The Best Devotions of Marilyn Meberg
Copyright © 2001 by Marilyn Meberg

Requests for information should be addressed to:
Zondervan, *Grand Rapids, Michigan 49530*

Library of Congress Cataloging-in-Publication Data

Meberg, Marilyn.
    The best devotions of Marilyn Meberg/Marilyn Meberg.
       p. cm.
    ISBN 0-310-24176-6
    1. Christian women—Prayer-books and devotions—English.
I. Title.
BV4844 .M43 2001
242—dc21   2001026578

All Scripture quotations, unless otherwise indicated, are from the *Holy Bible, New International Version* (NIV), © 1973, 1984 by the International Bible Society. Used by permission of Zondervan. All rights reserved.

Other Scripture quotations are from *New American Standard Bible* (NASB), © 1960, 1977 by the Lockman Foundation; *The Message* (MSG), © 1993, 1994, 1995 by Eugene H. Peterson; *The Living Bible* (TLB), © 1971 by Tyndale House Publishers; *The New Living Translation* (NLT), © 1996 By Tyndale Charitable Trust; and the *King James Version* (KJV).

All rights reserved. No part of this publication may be reproduced, stored in a retrieval system, or transmitted in any form or by any means—electronic, mechanical, photocopy, recording, or any other—except for brief quotations in printed reviews, without the prior permission of the publisher.

Published in association with the literary agency of Alive Communications, Inc., 7680 Goddard Street, Suite 200, Colorado Springs, CO 80920.

Interior design by Beth Shagene

Printed in the United States of America

01 02 03 04 05 06 07 08 /❖ DC/ 10 9 8 7 6 5 4 3 2 1

Taken from *Joy Breaks* by Patsy Clairmont, Barbara Johnson, Marilyn Meberg, Luci Swindoll, Sheila Walsh, and Thelma Wells. Copyright © 1997 by New Life Clinics. Used by permission of Zondervan.

Taken from *We Brake for Joy* by Patsy Clairmont, Barbara Johnson, Marilyn Meberg, Luci Swindoll, Sheila Walsh, and Thelma Wells. Copyright © 1998 by Women of Faith, Inc. Used by permission of Zondervan.

Taken from *Overjoyed!* by Patsy Clairmont, Barbara Johnson, Marilyn Meberg, Luci Swindoll, Sheila Walsh, and Thelma Wells. Copyright © 1999 by Women of Faith, Inc. Used by permission of Zondervan.

Taken from *Extravagant Grace* by Patsy Clairmont, Barbara Johnson, Marilyn Meberg, Luci Swindoll, Sheila Walsh, and Thelma Wells. Copyright © 2000 by Women of Faith, Inc. Used by permission of Zondervan.

Taken from *Boundless Love* by Patsy Clairmont, Barbara Johnson, Marilyn Meberg, Luci Swindoll, Sheila Walsh, and Thelma Wells. Copyright © 2000 by Women of Faith, Inc. Used by permission of Zondervan.

*I dedicate this book
of sweet memories and ponderings
to my darling son, Jeff, and
my equally darling daughter, Beth.
I love you!*

Contents

Foreword by Luci Swindoll

Next year I will have known Marilyn Meberg thirty years, and what wonderful years they've been. All this time we've been close friends. I knew her parents and her husband, I'm good friends with her children and grandchildren. We've laughed together, cried together, prayed together, traveled together, and been together when the other was up or down. The unity and harmony that pervades our relationship is one of my sweetest treasures.

Therefore, when I drew the straw that permitted me to write the foreword to *The Best Devotions of Marilyn Meberg,* I was thrilled. I hope I can do justice to this unique, delightful friend. Actually, I could write volumes about Marilyn, but since I'm allowed only a few paragraphs, I'll touch on the strongest aspects of her writing, which you will find repeatedly throughout this book.

I heard Marilyn speak long before I read her books. Even then, I was captivated. She has the three things I love most in a communicator:

> An exceptional use of the English language
> An unparalleled sense of humor
> An intimate relationship with the Lord

Look for these things as you read this book. They slide in and out of conversations, sentences, paragraphs, and one story after another. Sometimes you won't even know what hit you, you'll feel so at home with this gifted wordsmith.

The year I met Marilyn, she was teaching English at Biola University and occasionally we discussed her classes and students. How I wished *I* were one of them. She challenged young men and women to think associatively, question anything they didn't understand, and look for social commentary in novels, poetry, and essays. And as Marilyn talked about her work, it was like having a conversation with Charles Dickens. Her *words!* Oh my . . . they made me want to read those same books, and often I did, just to keep up with my new friend. We placed bets about proper usage of adjectives or nouns and debated sentence construction, always challenging each other to think creatively, enjoying the language with which we are blessed in this country.

And is Marilyn *funny?* Well, that gift alone would have kept me coming back for more even if she'd been the greatest dullard in the world . . . because I love to laugh. My maternal grandmother used to say, "A day is wasted if you don't fall over in a heap laughing," so when I got to know Marilyn that joy multiplied, and I was constantly falling in heaps. (She and my grandmother would have been great pals.)

Marilyn has the ability to see humor in the absurd, the off-center, the quirky, wacky ways of humankind. And most especially she laughs at herself—her own foibles and idiosyncrasies. Don't you love that in a person? Watch for these clever turns of phrases and confessions as you read along. In her devotionals Marilyn braids together threads of wonder, charm, beauty, enjoyment, and downright sidesplitting humor. Capturing the essence of real life situations, she invites us to laugh *and* to think.

Finally, you will discover Marilyn's devotionals to be filled with her love for the Lord, his Word, his ways, and his promise of providing for every one of us. As she relates stories about her family and friends you'll be blessed and challenged. For example, when Marilyn writes about calling upon God in her devotional entitled, "The Hair Prayer," it encourages us to bring him the concerns that to others might seem silly or unimportant. When she writes in "A Divine Prescription" about finding joy and laughter in the midst of sickness, it assures us that God promises to meet us in the same way. And "Smoke Travels" is a wonderful devotional on God's matchless grace, shown in such a unique way.

There are many words that describe Marilyn Meberg—outlandish, daring, bright, clever, verbal, appreciative . . . and the list goes on. But nothing quite captures it like *eloquent*. And that's the way she writes. In her persuasive, fluent manner, she takes the gift of life and frames it into a pleasing, interesting, and captivating work of art. Knowing Marilyn has enriched my life, and it will enrich yours too.

Croakings of Joy

Let me hear joy and gladness.
PSALM 51:8

Now that I'm living in the desert in a condominium, I haven't been in such proximity to other people since dorm life in college. And frankly, I love it! I like to be surrounded by people; I like to hear occasional plumbing sounds, human voices, and even know what my neighbors are watching on TV. (I don't always approve of their choices, but I suppose people have the right to be wrong on occasion.) I find all this closeness rather comforting. Plus I've also gotten some wonderful giggles as a result.

For example, my neighbors to the left (Bob and Julie) are warm, sociable people who love to laugh and entertain. Several days ago I noticed through the window (the window is directly behind my desk, so I occasionally swivel around just to keep in touch) that Bob was putzing around with a mechanical green frog that is supposed to croak when you get within two feet of it. It continues to croak until you leave its "croak space."

Apparently, this frog was not performing properly and in exasperation Bob called into the house to Julie, "This frog has truly croaked. It won't make a sound." I smiled at this clever pun and swiveled back to work.

Yesterday my friend Pat came over with her little dachshund, Mr. Hobbs, to go on our scheduled walk. As we came out the front door, Mr. Hobbs noticed Bob's green frog on the front stoop. Hobbs bristled, did his deep-throated growl (which never sounds threatening — he must hate that), and stealthily crept toward it. Not knowing that Bob had replaced the mechanically dead croaker with one that functioned, I was as startled as Mr. Hobbs when it started croaking loudly. Hobbs jumped straight into the air and dashed behind Pat for safety.

Last night, returning from a wild and woolly night at the movies, I made my uncertain way in the dark to my front door. I'd forgotten to leave the porch light on and apparently entered the croak zone unawares because my presence set the frog into a frenzy of croaking that did not stop until I got inside. I giggled to myself as I realized I would never be able to sneak in and out of my own house as long as this vigilant green frog was on duty.

This frog provides me with yet another example of my theory that the giggles in life usually come from little things. If we train ourselves to look for them, see them, and then giggle with them or even at them, we get a "perk." Seeing these potential breaks from routine sometimes requires that we adjust the lenses through which we see life. That adjustment can be as simple as heightening our awareness of the quirky and unusual around us. Giggle potential is everywhere; we just need to slow down long enough to see it.

Lord Jesus, without our knowledge of you and salvation from you, we would be unable to truly 'hear joy' or feel gladness. You are the source of our peace, the foundation upon which our security rests, and the inspiration for finding gladness in the dailyness of our lives. May we experience more God-given gladness as we celebrate the days you have ordained for us here on earth. Amen.

Ten Thousand Butterflies— Maybe More

How many are your works, O LORD! In wisdom
you made them all; the earth is full of your creatures.
PSALM 104:24

Last week I got one of those delicious "life perks" while driving to "Parents' Place" in Pacific Grove, California. Before I describe my perk, let me fill you in on a couple of tidbits of information.

My daughter, Beth, her golf-pro husband, Steve, and my adorable seventeen-month-old grandson, Ian, live in Carmel, California (a very long nine-hour drive from Grandma). Ever since Ian was six days old, Beth and he have gone to the neighboring town of Pacific Grove for a weekly meeting of moms and their little ones at Parents' Place. These little people have now graduated from Mama's arms to well-carpeted floors, and they lurch about babbling on play telephones, climb in little plastic chairs, and occasionally hit one another with whatever is at hand. Because I had attended the very first meeting when Ian was newborn, I was thrilled to go again and see how all these little persons have grown and developed. It was on our way there that I experienced the perk.

We were wending our way through several tree-canopied streets when I saw it: a road sign that read CAUTION: BUTTERFLY ZONE. I was utterly charmed but totally mystified.

"Beth, did you see that butterfly sign? What on earth does it mean? Is it for real? Why does one need to be cautious about butterflies? Are they hostile?"

She explained to me that Pacific Grove is one of the few migratory destinations in the world for the Monarch butterfly and that the area in which we were riding was one of their specific destinations.

"But why does that fact warrant a sign asking motorists to be cautious?"

"Mom, from the first of October until the end of November there can be literally thousands of butterflies swarming across the road on their way to the various groves of trees where they spend the winter. You could injure or even kill them."

Well, that image put me in a deep "think" that lasted at least twenty minutes. I was touched by the tender seriousness of this city's residents in preserving the well-being of these delicate and gorgeous creatures. In addition to being touched, I was sufficiently intrigued to call the Pacific Grove Chamber of Commerce later and learn more about their provision for the Monarchs.

I was told that there is a city ordinance that mandates punishment by a heavy fine for anyone caught hurting or interfering in any way with the safety of the butterflies. Also, each year on the second Saturday of October, every preschool and kindergarten child in town dresses up as a Monarch butterfly, and the whole city welcomes the returning Monarchs with a six-block parade. I asked my informant how many butterflies make their sometimes-1800-mile trek to Pacific Grove. She happily reported that thus far there were about ten thousand, but more would be coming. She concluded by pronouncing: "These butterflies are a very big deal to us." That statement and my recently acquired knowledge made my insides smile and go soft.

Creation is filled with stunning variety and exquisite beauty. The delicate, intricate, and fragile as well as the strong, mighty, and powerful testify sweetly to the richness of the Creator. It is crucial that we attend not only to the needs of the human beings that inhabit this earth, but also to the preservation of the countless creatures that contribute to the beauty and balance of our God-given environment. I need to be reminded that "in wisdom" he made them all, and a part of my reverencing him is my reverencing all the earth's creatures: humans, animals, flowers, trees, and, yes, the ten thousand butterflies hidden in those trees.

O Father, the God of all creation, enable me to revel in the works of your hands with a renewed vision and a protective enthusiasm. The earth is indeed "full of your creatures." In reverencing you, I also must reverence them. Amen.

Go For It!

So then, banish anxiety from your heart
and cast off the troubles of your body.
ECCLESIASTES 11:10

There's a certain love of the risky and wild in me that rarely needs encouragement. One of those more delicious fulfillments of my wild side occurred years ago when I was teaching English at Biola University.

On a Saturday afternoon preceding the beginning of winter semester, Beth and I drove over to the school so I could put my class syllabuses on the secretary's desk for typing and distribution to classes on Monday morning. I needed to get into my office, but the building was locked. That meant I had to walk all the way over to the administration building and pick up a master key.

I grumbled and snorted my way over there, asked for a key to the building, was told I had to leave my driver's license, agreed to those peculiar terms, made my way back to my office, left the syllabuses, and was irritated that I had to walk all the way back to the administration building to return the key.

At the time of this story, I was driving a little blue Fiat convertible, which I adored. I experienced an indescribable sense of euphoria whizzing freely about in that little convertible. Because of its size I was able to zip in and out of spaces prohibited to the larger, more traditional and sedate cars. One of my delights was to experience just how many places I could go that bigger cars could not.

Looking fondly now at my little car in the Biola parking lot, where Beth was waiting patiently for me, I got one of those deliciously wild and risky ideas. The Biola buildings are connected by a network of sidewalks that crisscross all over campus. As I walked those various sidewalks during a typical class day, I often mused about the width of the walks and whether my Fiat would fit on them. *What a fabulous time to find out*, I thought.

Leaping into the car, I announced to Beth that we were in a hurry and then pulled onto the sidewalk leading to the administration building. We were a perfect fit: on either side of the tires was only an inch or two of sidewalk to spare. With an exuberant whoop I exclaimed, "Beth, look at what a tidy fit we are. Don't you love this?" She shot me a look of withering disapproval that only a sixteen-year-old can muster and chided, "Mom, you are not for real!"

Undaunted, I buzzed forward. But my euphoria was short-lived as I heard a jarringly loud honk behind me. To my amazement there was a big, fat Biola security car poised by the sidewalk entrance; the driver was motioning me to return to the parking lot. I was stunned. Where on earth had he come from?

Well, this is a bit sticky, I mused to myself. *Here I am, a faculty member, jauntily driving on the sidewalk, knowing full well I should not be. What do I do? I'm where I'm not supposed to be, doing what I'm not supposed to be doing. It can't get any worse. So why stop?*

My pertinacity inspired the security guy to turn on his siren and red lights and to pull onto the sidewalk in hot pursuit. I noticed in my side mirror that his tires hung over both sides of the sidewalk, leaving unsightly tread marks in the grass. *He should be ashamed of himself,* I thought. I also thought I'd better stop.

When he asked where I was going, I told him I was heading over to the administration building to pick up my driver's license. That didn't sit well with him. When he asked why I was on the sidewalk, I told him I was in midlife crisis and that sometimes I got irresistible urges. He wasn't responsive to that either.

I told this story not long afterward to a gathering of women, and one of them sent me a bumper sticker that read: "If you don't like the way I drive, get off the sidewalk!"

This brand of risky living may not be to your taste, but let me encourage you to stretch to the degree that feels safe to you. It may be no more wild than eating dessert before dinner. You might graduate to something like wearing your wedding dress to the grocery store. Whatever it is, consider the degree of risky and wild you can tolerate, and then go for it!

Lord, teach us to "banish anxiety from our hearts and cast off the troubles of our bodies." Thank you for the assurance of your love for us, which releases us to live out joyful impulses. Create within us a lightness of being that comes from knowing you. Amen.

Put Another Log on the Fire

My people will live in peaceful dwelling places,
in secure homes, in undisturbed places of rest.
ISAIAH 32:18

In spite of my oft-spoken philosophy of freedom to enjoy the moment, take a risk, or get out of a rut, I'm amazed at my own "rut-think" that periodically takes over. For instance, this past weekend I spoke at a pre-Christmas conference at Forest Home Christian Conference Center. I adore Forest Home and have been honored to fill a guest speaker spot for them many times through the years.

As I entered my little cabin, "The Biltmore," to put my stuff away and gather my thoughts, I noticed a most compelling arrangement of firewood all set up in the gorgeous stone fireplace. It appeared to need nothing more than a match. There was a bone-chilling cold in the air, but it was really too late to start a fire.

The next day, having spoken twice in the morning, I came back to my little Biltmore for a few delicious hours to myself. Looking again at that carefully laid arrangement of wood, I thought how much I would love doing a little writing, resting, and thinking utterly blank thoughts with a fire crackling in the background. But as I examined the wood more closely, I could see no way to start a fire. There was no paper, no kindling, no evidence whatsoever that a fire could start, short of rubbing two sticks together. I thought, *Oh, well, Marilyn, you don't need a fire. The cabin is warm. You're very comfortable as you are. Give up the idea.*

I hearkened back to the days of my youth when we sat around our stone fireplace in Amboy, Washington. There were two especially severe storms one winter that knocked out our electricity so that the fireplace was our only source of heat and our only source of fuel for cooking. I don't remember anything of the obvious inconvenience; I only remember feeling that I was a pioneer, braving the elements with courage and fortitude. (Of course, my courage and fortitude were totally dependent upon that of my parents—a fact that never occurred to me then.)

Overwhelmed with nostalgia, I determined I simply must have a fire in the fireplace! But how? I had noticed a tidy pile of wood on the little enclosed porch, so I poked around out there for a possible clue as to how to start my longed-for fire. Then it appeared! A two-gallon jug with the barely legible word DIESEL felt-penned on the side sat slightly behind the woodpile. So this is what one uses to start a fire! But wait a minute ... how does one use diesel? It then seemed sensible to me that one simply needed to sprinkle, douse, or drench the wood with the diesel. I elected to drench the wood rather than sprinkle or douse.

As I was getting ready to touch the drenched wood with the lighter, I stopped abruptly and pondered, *What if this wood explodes into an uncontrollable inferno because I should have sprinkled rather than drenched? What if I destroy the entire conference center with but a flick of my lighter wand? I don't know anything about diesel except that it smells bad and cars that swallow it don't move fast. Well, hey ... maybe a diesel fire won't move fast either. Go for it, Marilyn!*

When the drenched wood and flame united in one beautiful moment of contained harmony, I was euphoric! All afternoon I sat in front of that crackling blaze, occasionally throwing another log on the fire and getting in touch with my nearly forgotten pioneer roots of courage and fortitude.

What if I had elected to douse my idea of a fire instead of dousing the wood with diesel? I would have never had that nearly three hours of soul-satisfying reverie. I nearly gave up the idea because I thought maybe I shouldn't risk it.

This may sound a bit naïve, but some of my greatest spiritual moments have been inspired by the unexpected and the simple. I can't tell you what a wonderful afternoon of Jesus-chat I experienced in front of my mildly risky fire. I truly felt as if I were in a God-given "peaceful dwelling place ... in an undisturbed place of rest." All of that and a crackling fire too.

Dear God, I love the fact that wherever I am, you are there too. You are with me in front of the fire as well as in church. You are with me in the night as well as in the morning. You are with me in times of sadness and in times of gladness. May I never be in such a rut that I limit this awareness of your creative presence. Amen.

Yahoo!

For in Christ all the fullness of the Deity lives in bodily form,
and you have been given fullness in Christ,
who is the head over every power and authority.

COLOSSIANS 2:9–10

"Now do I assume, Pat, that you've signed up for these lessons to improve your skills in skating around the rink?"

"Well, sure, I need to improve in that too, but that's not why I signed up for lessons."

Debbie, a figure-skating instructor who would still be skating professionally if a back injury had not interfered with her career, looked at Pat warmly and said, "Tell me what you hope to learn in your lessons."

"I want to skate faster, do spins, and maybe ultimately a double or triple axel."

Debbie sucked in her breath, quickly appraised Pat's fifty-eight-year-old body, and with an enthusiastic nod said, "Okay . . . let's get to work!"

I met Pat Wenger at Pepperdine University where we were both studying to complete our master's degree in counseling psychology. Like me, she had been a teacher and was embarking on a second career. Because of many personal similarities, we immediately became good friends. Ultimately, we shared a suite of offices together when we went into private practice. Pat lives in the desert part-time, so when she's here we get together frequently. She's the one who enthusiastically sells my tapes at the Joyful Journey conferences.

Yielding to an inner itch, Pat bought ice skates a year ago and now skates every Monday morning at our local mall rink. This time is set aside for just those in the skating club; kids and others are not allowed. Pat had not been on ice skates since she was ten years old, but each time she glides the ice now, there's increased assurance and a growing desire to do what was denied her as a child. She wants to learn to figure skate: not just go around and around the rink but occasionally twirl and jump!

Though much of me lauds her wild and risky aspirations, there's another part of me that feels nervous for her safety. With my typically generous spirit I asked her how she could sell my tapes if she became a quadriplegic from one too many spins. She told me she would stop short of that and just go for the paraplegic designation so she could at least point.

There is an undeniable glow that radiates from Pat for hours after she's been skating. Obviously something is released in her as she harmonizes her skates and body on that slippery ice. I've seen that same glow on the faces of a darling couple who are in their eighties and who also skate at the rink every Monday morning. I don't see them jumping and twirling, though. When I pointed that out to Pat, her response was that when she reaches her eighties she won't twirl and jump anymore either.

I rather envy all this. I have never been on ice skates in my life and have no desire to start now. There is, however, a certain freedom and joy that comes from the mastery of something seemingly beyond our abilities. The idea of always playing it safe, never venturing out of our comfort zone, and refusing to broaden the borders of our experience is stultifying.

That being the case, I've decided to sign up for line-dancing lessons. Don't call me on Tuesday nights because I'll be at the Lariat Club in Palm Springs. Yahoo!

Because of you, Lord Jesus, I have the fullness, the richness, the joyfulness of your total deity within my being. Because you have given me the gift of salvation through your death on the cross, I have been set free from the weight of sin. I can enter into new experiences with ease and gratitude and give you praise for these earthly pleasures. Amen.

A Castle in Italy

> "If you, then, though you are evil, know how to give
> good gifts to your children, how much more will your Father
> in heaven give good gifts to those who ask him!"
>
> MATTHEW 7:11

You want to get married in Italy?! Good grief, Beth, why? No one would be able to attend—what about your friends? Don't you want more people to be there cheering you on than just our small immediate family? Mercy . . . Italy!"

Slowly, very slowly, Beth began to sell me on the idea. Her logic turned out to be pretty convincing! Steve's parents were going to be in Udine, Italy, for six months. Steve and Beth reasoned that getting married during his parents' stay there would be perfect timing. After some investigation, I realized that flying there for a small wedding would probably be even less expensive than a full-blown wedding in the States. I began to soften.

But the clincher came when Beth explained, "You know, Mom, I've never liked doing what everyone else does—it's boring. And you also know I've never wanted a traditional wedding. But more important, Mom, Dad isn't here to walk me down the aisle. Somehow being in an entirely different environment will make that reality less painful for me."

That did it: I was sold.

Beth and Steve were married in the Castello Formentini in Gorizia, Italy, on November 28, 1991. This fifteenth-century castle is utterly spectacular. Located on the border of what was once Yugoslavia, it has been renovated into a resort hotel complete with golf course. Interestingly enough, the renovations have not tampered in the slightest with its fifteenth-century charm.

After a sweetly Christ-centered service performed by the pastor from Udine, we retired to a stone-walled banquet room complete with gorgeous works of art and a crackling fire. We and the twenty other guests embarked upon a traditional Italian wedding feast that went on for five hours. All of this may sound a bit ostentatious, but if you can believe it, the dinner cost less than if we had had the American version of slightly stale wedding cake with chocolate mousse filling, preceded by cucumber and cream cheese canapés.

Watching Beth's radiant face in the midst of these magical festivities pleased me enormously. I thought how glad I was for her love of the different and unique and how grateful I was that God had so beautifully orchestrated this memorable event. After all, he too loves the different and unique, and he wants us to be true to our own peculiarities. God planted in Beth desires for her wedding ceremony that were uniquely her own, and I'm glad I honored them.

I am so grateful for God's provision not only for our basic needs but also for those that are occasionally far outside the norm. Sometimes I forget the sweet truth that God's Father-heart delights in giving good gifts to his children.

Heavenly Father, thank you for those gifts you give us that are out of the ordinary and far beyond our expectations. There is no limit to your creativity, no limit to your generosity, and no limit to your pleasure in being our Father. Thank you that I am the daughter of the eternal King. Amen.

A Mirror Image

So God created man in his own image,
in the image of God he created him;
male and female he created them.
GENESIS 1:27

As an only child I never experienced the mirroring that often comes with having a sibling—you know, that catching a body gesture or tone of voice that wasn't mine but still looked or sounded a lot like mine. My childhood fantasy was to have an identical twin. In fact, I used to pretend I had a twin; in my imagination we talked alike, looked alike, and behaved alike.

I don't know the source of my desire for a twin other than the sense of isolation I occasionally felt as an only child in small rural communities. I wonder if in some way I thought an identical twin would validate my existence, assure me that "Yes, you are who you are, and, yes, you are there." (This sounds a bit neurotic, Marilyn.)

I thought I'd outgrown my "mirror-neurosis" until I met my Aunt Wilda for the first time about six years ago. She is my father's "baby sister." We don't look anything alike, but what startled me into a kind of primal recognition was her approach to life. As we were having dinner together in my home, Aunt Wilda, at my request, began to tell some of her early life experiences.

Her unbridled enthusiasm, zest for minor mischief, as well as preference for the fast-paced life stirred in me a sense of having met my twin. What cinched that sense was her admission of her driving record. With twinkling Irish blue eyes she told me she was not proud of the fact that she continually got speeding tickets; but, she said, "Marilyn, how in the world do people manage to stay within the speed limit? It's simply too slow!" Responding with a hug of instant kinship, I began to share my own driving history and penchant for speeding.

Her response to my string of confessions was to pronounce, "There's no hope for you, Marilyn. Let me tell you why." She then told me how, shortly before Christmas one year, she had been pulled over by a policeman just outside her hometown of Toronto, Canada. He checked her license and insurance papers, then asked if she knew how fast she'd been going. Her response was, "Well, not as fast as I'd like. There are simply too many cars on the road!"

"Mrs. Johnson, I see by our computerized printout that you have quite a record of speeding tickets."

"Yes, I do, but that's not because I want them."

"What are the chances of your simply driving more slowly?"

"Probably not good."

"May I ask how old you are, Mrs. Johnson?"

"Eighty-two."

"I suppose it wouldn't do much good if I gave you a ticket then, would it?"

"I doubt it."

He patted her shoulder, told her to take care of herself, and said he hoped he would never have occasion to stop her again. She cheerfully replied, "I wouldn't mind that a bit. You are a lovely young man."

Concluding her story, she explained, "So you see, Marilyn, some things never change. You simply have 'speed genes'; you were probably born with them!"

I do not for one moment condone speeding and then excusing it by claiming "I can't help it; it runs in the family." My point here is that there is sometimes an almost mysterious sense of the "aha" when we meet people that seem to so perfectly mirror portions of ourselves. That experience provides a companionable feeling of oneness and kinship.

What is even more mysterious and provides an even greater sense of the "aha" is the fact that we have been created in God's image. Jesus, who said "if you have seen me you have seen the Father," experienced every feeling, every nuance of emotion, every temptation on this earth that you and I do. If this truth is a reality to us, we can't help but be humbled by his graciousness in continually working to conform us to his image. What an awesome privilege that in our rebellious state he loves us and welcomes us always as part of the family—not because of what we do, but because of what he did on the cross.

When we look into the mirror, may we see more and more of him.

Lord, what a mark of love and grace to be created in your image! And what grace you extend to us as you call us "children of God." Enable us to talk like you, act like you, and even think like you as your Spirit refines us and molds us ever more into your image. Amen.

"The Plan"

In him we were also chosen, having been predestined
according to the plan of him who works out everything
in conformity with the purpose of his will.

EPHESIANS 1:11

During my last visit to Beth and Steve's house in
Carmel, little Ian, Beth, and I drove to the neighboring town of Monterey so Beth could see Dr. Walker, her
ob-gyn. Why? Because she's pregnant!

Am I excited?

Does the sun shine daily in Palm Desert? I'm thrilled
to death!

This is cutting it a bit close in some ways, though,
because Ian will only be twenty-three months old when
"she" arrives. I'm sure Ian's initial response will be to
pack his little suitcase in disgust and move to Grandma's.

As they have talked over the unexpected timing of her
pregnancy, Beth and Steve have both had to walk through
a few steps before relinquishing their agendas. Both feel
Ian is a bit too young to have to relinquish his position as
King Baby. The timing is not great for them financially;
both had hoped to get a bit ahead or, more realistically,
just catch up before another baby hit the scene. And Beth
wanted one more year to see that Ian is as grounded as
possible in this world of good times and bad before facing

the inevitable sibling rivalry that comes when new kids arrive on board.

I don't think there's a human being schlepping through life that does not have a "plan" for how things will be. "We'll have two babies, a boy and a girl, who will be three years apart, and then after that..." There also is not a human being alive who has not experienced unexpected interruptions or unwanted alterations to "the plan." The one constant in life is change. Nothing stays the same, and the same is usually changed to something we don't recognize. We are in a continual cycle of beginnings, middles, and endings, and not always in that order. If we habitually resist that reality, we'll generally be distressed with life.

When I finally internalized the plan-shattering reality that Ken had cancer and that cancer was going to kill him, my mind reeled with a million arguments. "Now wait a minute . . . we were supposed to retire in ten years and take trips . . . I was going to surprise him with a golf cart on our thirtieth wedding anniversary . . . we're supposed to indulge and spoil grandchildren together . . . Ken was supposed to make gourmet dinners every Saturday night for the rest of our lives . . . Ken was supposed to always do the income taxes so I wouldn't ever even have to look at the forms . . . we were supposed to hold each other when we were cold, lonely, or simply loving. What about all that stuff, God?"

I have every invitation from the Father to fuss and complain about "the plan." However, if I stay in the fuss-complain mode and refuse to relinquish my agenda, I'll never have peace.

How do we truly give up our agendas? How do we genuinely say, "Not my will but yours, Lord"? For me, the answer to that question is found in my understanding and acceptance of God's sovereignty. God "works out everything in conformity with the purpose of his will." All happenings on this earth and in my life are worked out in conformity with his purpose — not mine, but his. God's sovereignty is not an attribute of God but a prerogative of God. He does what he does.

What softens my response to what in my human understanding could seem autocratic of God is to remember the nature of God. The nature of God is love. For a rich reminder of this attribute of his, just look up all the verses on his love for you in a Bible concordance. It will soften your resistance and inspire a reciprocal love for him. His love is simply too great and too all-encompassing to step around.

Based on that love platform is the realization that I am not incidental in the grand scheme of things. In Ephesians 1:4–5, the apostle Paul tells us, "For he chose us in him before the creation of the world to be holy and blameless in his sight. In love he predestined us to be adopted as his sons through Jesus Christ, in accordance with his pleasure and will."

I am not an afterthought. All God's love-inspired preplanning for each of us is not haphazard or impersonal. His timing may throw me or his sovereign plan may grieve me, but I am always sheltered in his sovereign hand. Can I rest in that? Can I quit resisting that? Not always, but that's my humanness interfering with my acceptance of his divineness.

Are Beth and Steve having an ill-timed baby? Not according to Ephesians 1:11. Did Ken die prematurely? Not according to Ephesians 1:11. Perhaps the more appropriate question is "Will I accept his sovereign will in my life?" If I do, or when I do, I will have experienced his sovereign plan for my life.

Lord, how frequently and mindlessly we kick against the very constraints you put in place for our growth and refinement. Remind those of us who get so caught up with the earthly that to do so is to miss the heavenly. Your plan for each of us is not one of earthly ease but of heavenly peace. Amen.

Mine!

Good will come to him who is generous and lends freely,
who conducts his affairs with justice.

PSALM 112:5

My little grandson Ian had picked up a phrase that neither Beth nor Steve had taught him, so it came as a surprise when he started saying "no way" instead of his customary "no" when he wished to express a negative response. I thought it was a deliciously fun way to express resistance, and I started saying it along with him.

What intrigued me about his phrase was the way he said it. He had no anger or belligerence in his voice; it was always said with a quiet but plaintive tone as if he assumed his protest would go unheeded if he didn't make himself perfectly clear.

The morning that Beth, Ian, and I went to see Dr. Walker was one of those priceless times when his little "no way" protest took everyone off guard. Beth had been experiencing a nagging cough that had persisted since the beginning of her pregnancy, so in addition to the two-month pregnancy checkup, Dr. Walker's advice about the cough was solicited.

Beth was sitting on the exam table with Ian perched uncertainly on her lap. He wasn't sure what was going to go on in that room, but whatever it was, it was obvious he didn't have peace about it. His little face was puckered in pensive disapproval as Beth described her cough, how long she'd had it, and so on. Dr. Walker put his stethoscope against her back and told her to take several deep breaths. Then he moved the stethoscope from her back and slipped it down the front of her blouse. That was too much for Ian. With startling clarity he pronounced "No way" and tried to push Dr. Walker's hand away. The doctor was stunned by these words from the baby he had delivered just seventeen months before. Chuckling, he said, "Getting too close to your milk supply, aren't I, little guy?"

Beth suggested I take Ian outside, since it was only going to get worse. He wouldn't leave the room with me until Dr. Walker pretended to leave first.

As Ian and I repeatedly marched up and down the twenty-four steps outside the medical building, I thought about how the need to relinquish is a relentless part of daily living. Here's this tiny little fellow already faced with the need to relinquish his mama to some brutish doctor back in "that room." And in another seven months there will be more relinquishing when his baby sister arrives and takes over the house as well as the milk supply.

Our relinquishing may be as benign as giving up a parking spot to the person who feels certain she got there first. Or it may appear more crucially in our relationships: possibly a husband who seems to spend more time with the job than the family. It may well be that these priorities need to be examined, but it may also be good to consider how balanced we are in our expectations of each other's work time. Maybe we need to relinquish our inordinate need to have a spouse or a particular friend constantly at our side, listening to us, doing for us, and providing security for us. Or maybe we have parents who, now that they've retired, seem always to be off somewhere on a cruise or involved in some other activity that prevents them from being as available to us as we'd like. Perhaps we need to relinquish them to their hard-won freedom from the responsibilities they've carried all their lives.

Then of course there's that really tough one called relinquishing the children. Relinquishing them to marry someone we wouldn't choose, or to live too far away for frequent visits. Perhaps a son or daughter wants to attend a college or university that isn't our first choice. Do we need to relinquish our power and control and encourage them in their own choices?

Often we grasp too tightly whatever is a source of security for us. That usually indicates some early deprivation in our background, and we'd be wise to take a look at that and see if we're trying to get others to meet our needs. It's not the job of others to do that, unless of course we're seventeen months old and lunch appears to be in jeopardy.

What are you holding too tightly? What can't you relinquish, thinking that your next meal depends on it? Perhaps you and the Lord could make that a prayer project, with your ultimate goal being the ability to say "Whatever, Lord."

Lord Jesus, you remind us that you honor a generous heart and one that lends freely. May we learn to give more and demand less. Enable us to do more letting go and less holding on. May we simply yield to your sweet spirit of generosity and in so doing relinquish that part of us that fears not being in control. Take the reins from our grasping grip and teach us to rest in that release. Amen.

To Bean or Not to Bean

Know that the Lord is God.
It is he who made us, and we are his.
PSALM 100:3

When Beth and Steve decided to get married in Italy, I realized I would need a coat! This southern California damsel did not even own a winter coat because she rarely needed one. But, I reasoned, if we were all going to traipse to Europe in the dead of winter, do the tourist thing by going to Paris first, and then do the wedding thing, I needed to ward off the potential of freezing to death.

L. L. Bean is a mail-order house in Freeport, Maine, whose catalogs I pore over regularly. I love that place! Almost all of my wool-cashmere blazers have come from there, and my turtlenecks and sweaters as well. There's something irresistibly fun about simply picking up the phone, calling the toll-free number, and chatting with one of their amiable salespersons as I give my order. I always find out how cold it is there, and then of course point out that we in southern California are basking in seventy-degree sunshine. (That's an unattractive side of me I'm not proud of, but I seem to continue to express it in spite of my disapproval.)

What better place to buy a warm coat for Europe than L. L. Bean! I was tremendously rushed that fall anyway, and the ease of simply ordering my coat without leaving home was wonderful.

When my bright blue quilted goose-down coat with optional zippered hood arrived, I felt ready for any temperature. It claimed to be lightweight for packing as well as wearing, and indeed it was. In fact, it proved so efficiently to retain my body heat, I never once felt cold in spite of freezing temperatures in Paris. I basically just cooed and smiled from the depths of my goose-down cocoon the entire three days we "did" Paris prior to going on to Italy.

Since then, this coat has cuddled and cocooned me many times: sitting on cold bleachers waiting for the Rose Bowl Parade to start, traveling to other cities whose temperatures nearly rival those of wintertime Paris, and then again just last week when we all went to New York for Thanksgiving. (I'd have died without her encompassing warmth while standing rinkside at Rockefeller Center.)

Perhaps now that I have so drawn you into my inordinate affection as well as appreciation of "Bean," you can possibly understand how startled I was to suddenly realize one morning as we all walked down West 75th Street to Amsterdam Avenue that no one in New York was wearing a bright blue quilted goose-down coat except me. Everyone was wearing a long black, brown, or tan wool coat. On the heels of this realization came a delayed flashback. I thought, *I don't remember anyone in Paris wearing a bright blue Bean either.*

I caught my reflection in a window as we hunched our way down Amsterdam Avenue to Sarabeth's for breakfast. *You know, Marilyn, you really look like a walking sleeping bag. I hate to tell you that, but you stick out in a crowd. There are no other walking sleeping bags in all of New York!* I was crushed.

After we'd given our breakfast order I turned to my son and said, "Jeff, I want your absolute, honest response. Do you like my coat?"

Jeff stared at me for a minute and then eyeballed the crush of not only my coat but the coats of Pat and Carla on the seat beside me. He said, "You mean the Bean?"

"Yeah . . . the Bean."

"Well, Mom, because of your happy attachment to her in Paris, I really care only that you continue to be pleased with her."

I looked closely at him to be sure he wasn't doing that Ken Meberg thing. "Jeff, what do you think of my Bean?"

"Mom, um . . . she's great for certain places and occasions."

"Jeff, is she good for New York?"

"Probably not, Mom."

"Jeff, was she good for Paris?"

"She kept you warm . . . but otherwise no, Mom — she belongs somewhere else."

I looked at my gorgeous, fashion-plate daughter in law and said nothing. She too had the grace to say nothing.

My dear friend Pat, whose fidelity to truth-telling is often a challenge to me, offered, "I can tell you the exact place where Bean is appropriate."

Perking up, I asked, "Where?"

"She would be appropriate for you to wear for duck hunting. You know . . . those places where people lie low and then rise up from the marshes with guns pointed and shoot at ducks who suddenly fly out of nowhere."

I stared at her in total disbelief. "Pat, that's a terrible image. I can't imagine ever lying low to shoot a duck."

"Well, if you change your mind, you've got the coat for it!"

Fortunately our food arrived, and I settled into my Florentine omelette with extra-crisp bacon on the side. The subject of my Bean didn't come up again.

I must admit there was a slight decrease in my usual ebullience as we went about our activities following breakfast. I was busy settling the Bean issue. So what if I were the only walking bright blue quilted person in New York, or Paris, or Amboy for that matter! Why do I have to mirror everyone else's subdued earth-tone wool look? I don't! I love my Bean! I'm cozy and warm in my Bean . . . and as Jeff pointed out, "We can always find you in a crowd!"

What more could one ask from a coat? That settled it: There would be no severing of my relationship with Bean. She stays, and so do I. Nestled beneath several layers of lightweight goose down, I continued our New York activities, secure in the knowledge that I was the only genuinely warm person in the entire city!

Isn't it remarkable how uncomfortable we can become if we don't blend in to our environment? But without God-given uniqueness, everything would look the same, taste the same, and feel the same. What a bore! And what a loss.

May we learn, Lord Jesus, how dearly you love uniqueness and variety. Thank you that we all have different preferences and that there is no one quite like us on the earth. May we be pleased with our individuality, as you are pleased. Amen.

Two Plus Two Equals What?

Before I formed you in the womb I knew you.
JEREMIAH 1:5

I believe the first soul-thud recognition of my enormous math deficit hit me at the age of ten. I had been placed in an accelerated math class by a teacher who erroneously assumed I belonged there. I suppose that assumption was based upon the fact that I was doing fine in accelerated reading and writing classes.

I was vaguely aware that the fog rolled in whenever I caught sight of a number, but in that advanced class the density of the fog was so great I couldn't even make out who was sitting in front of me. My pitiful performance soon caught the attention of the teacher, and I was "decelerated" to a class of other fog-enshrouded children.

Though this was a relief to me in that the pressure to perform was lessened, from that point on I began to question my own adequacy. Thoughts like *teachers think you're smart, but then they find out you're not* loomed in my mind. I wondered how I could be so comfortable with words and so dense with numbers. Something, I assumed, was obviously wrong with my brain.

As I grew older and my dismal performance with numbers endured, I compensated by avoiding them as much as possible. By the time I entered college I felt relieved that math could go its way and I would go the opposite. I got a B.A. degree in English and to my knowledge never encountered a number the entire four years!

When our son Jeff was about two years old, I was a bit restless and felt the need for stimulation beyond high chairs, sandboxes, and tot trikes. Ken suggested I enroll in the graduate program at California State University, located in our town of Fullerton, and begin a master's degree in English. The idea was to take just one class each semester (one night a week) until I finished. There was no rush; I was just there for fun. What a great idea!

I soon learned, however, that there was a major challenge to be faced along with this aspiration: It was called the Graduate Record Exam. Not only would I be tested in those areas in which I had always excelled, but my math skills (or lack of them) would be tested as well.

I well remember sitting in a hot stuffy room, staring dumbfounded at pages and pages of math questions. Predictably, the fog came rolling in. "Now wait a minute, Marilyn. Don't give in to the old feeling of inadequacy. What you need to do is not bother reading the questions; they only confuse you. Since you merely have to black in either A, B, C, or D for each answer, simply construct a pattern. Mark a few A's, zip over to a few D's, balance the design with some scattered B's and C's, and see if you like the look of it. If not, change the pattern entirely: Do all A's, then all B's, and skip D's altogether!" That plan lifted my spirits enormously, and I got right to work on a pleasing pattern.

When the computerized results were mailed to our house weeks later, I of course couldn't make sense of the various percentages, but as Ken was interpreting them for me he began to laugh almost uncontrollably when he got to the math results. "Marilyn, there are actually three percent of the graduate population who scored lower in math than you did!"

"Really. . ." I said with mounting confidence. "You mean there are actually people who took that math part who did more poorly than I?"

"Absolutely, Marilyn . . . good for you!"

I pondered that happy news for a few minutes and then asserted with genuine compassion, "Those people should never have read the questions. That's probably why they didn't do as well as I did."

It has taken me some time to come to terms with the fact that I simply do not, never did, and never will feel comfortable in the presence of a number. However, for years I longed to be like everyone else in the world who, I perceived, could add a column of numbers so quickly that drool gathered in the corners of my mouth as I watched.

I simply do not have a numerical gift. I do, however, provide endless merriment for my friends as I valiantly try to calculate the tip from a lunch tab or stare blankly at the dinner table wondering why there are only five place settings while six people are waiting to be seated. I am as consistent in my deficit as Los Angeles smog. People can count on me. I have finally embraced my deficit with a reluctant warmth. After all, there's something to be said for consistent inability: It makes others feel secure.

Lord Jesus, I am who I am by your loving design. Help me to accept my weaknesses as well as my strengths. Help me, too, to embrace myself in my totality as you embrace me, knowing I cannot do what was not ordained for me. May I contentedly serve you, love you, and luxuriate in what you empower me to do in your name and for your sake. Amen.

The Greatest "Joy Break"

And what a difference between man's sin
and God's forgiveness!
ROMANS 5:15 TLB

Our first home was one that pleased Ken and me enormously. We loved our little fenced-in backyard and felt confident about the safety of both Jeff and Beth as they trundled about in it, often without need of our direct supervision.

On either side of the walkway leading to the front door was an area of decorative small rocks. Jeff loved to play in there with his Tonka trucks, creating roads and garages for his fleet of vehicles. Ken had attempted to impress upon Jeff's four-year-old mind the importance of keeping the rocks out of the grass because of the damage it would do to his lawnmower. In fact, Ken explained to Jeff that he was solely responsible for keeping the grass clear of rocks even if it were his friends and not Jeff who, in a burst of driving frenzy, managed to spew rocks into the grass.

One Friday morning as Jeff and I were bringing groceries into the house I noticed some rocks strewn about the grass area near the front door. I suggested to Jeff that he would need to get out there and remove them since Daddy would be mowing the next day. Jeff was indignant at the suggestion. "I didn't get those rocks in there; Nell did!"

"It doesn't matter who got them there, sweetheart. It's your job to keep the grass clear. That's Daddy's deal with you."

"That's not right . . . I didn't do it."

"I'm sorry, Jeff, but you still need to clear the grass whether it feels fair to you or not."

Jeff was always a mild-mannered little fellow and not the least prone to fits and fights. He trudged resolutely outside, but from his body language I could see he was laboring under a burden of victimization.

The kitchen window was open, and I could hear him muttering to himself as he sifted through the grass removing rocks. I was enormously curious to know the contents of his muttering so I leaned in the direction of the window. "I'm just like Jesus. I'm just like Jesus. I'm just like Jesus."

That was the last thing I expected to hear. What in the world was going on in his little mind? I decided to go outside and help him with the rock detail and, while there, ask him if he would talk about how he was just like Jesus. At first he would neither mutter nor talk to me. Finally, with my prodding, he retorted, "Well, Jesus never did anything bad, and he got punished. That's just the same as me!"

I enveloped his troubled little face with my eyes and then swooped him into my arms. He didn't cry, but I did.

Jeff's theology was a bit off, but we didn't go into it then. It is true that Jesus "who knew no sin" died that I, born in sin, might have eternal life. That is a difficult truth to comprehend at times. I love the clarity with which The Living Bible expresses this in Romans 5:15–17:

> For this one man, Adam, brought death to many through his sin. But this one man, Jesus Christ, brought forgiveness to many through God's mercy.

Adam's one sin brought the penalty of death to many, while Christ freely takes away many sins and gives glorious life instead. The sin of this one man, Adam, caused death to be king over all, but all who will take God's gift of forgiveness and acquittal are kings of life because of this one man, Jesus Christ.

Some years later, these regenerating truths became more clear to Jeff. Ultimately he came to understand that we not only identify with the sufferings of Christ, but we are set free because of the sufferings of Christ. What colossal good news!

As you are reading this book and contemplating the Jesus about whom we speak, I pray that you too know him personally. Without that precious relationship it is impossible to know the greatest "joy break" of all.

Lord Jesus, you who set us free from all the sin and condemnation that came upon the world through disobedience, we thank you. We thank you for our salvation; we thank you for our freedom; we thank you that there is no condemnation to those who are in Christ Jesus. We thank you that our acceptance of you as Savior means we are securely held in your embrace now and forever. Amen.

Coloring the Night Away

But the rich have many friends.
PROVERBS 14:20

Last night Pat and I had agreed to spend the evening together engaged in some wild and woolly activity yet to be determined. As we discussed various options I became increasingly aware of my fatigue from a very demanding week. From that fatigue came a most soothing, novel, and appealing idea.

I announced to Pat: "I want to buy crayons and a coloring book and spend the evening coloring." She stared at me for a minute trying to hide the look of incredulity on her face. Then, assuming her best therapist voice, she asked what kind of coloring book would please me and how many crayons I wanted. Pretending not to notice her clinical tone, I said I wanted at least twenty-four different colored crayons and that I would know the coloring book when I saw it.

With a kindly affirmation from Pat that spending the evening coloring might indeed be pleasant, she agreed to the plan. She did ask, however, if I thought smoking cigars while we colored would add a dimension of the adult to our activity. Since neither of us have the faintest notion of even how to smoke — much less a cigar — we quickly gave up that idea as not only impractical but unappealing as well.

True to expectation I found the perfect coloring book for me. It was called *The Huckleberry Finn Coloring Book*. *Huckleberry Finn* has always been one of my favorite novels, and I was instantly gratified by my purchase. Pat chose a coloring book of Disney characters that I thought was a bit beneath her level of sophistication, but I didn't think it would be kind to say so.

Armed with my new coloring book and a box of twenty-four crayons (Pat had to buy her own; I told her I absolutely would not share mine), I settled down to one of the most soothing and delightful evenings I've had in ages. While I determined the perfect color combination for the Widow Douglas's dress as well as the apron of her sister Miss Watson, we listened to Christmas music. Even though it wasn't yet Thanksgiving, and in spite of feeling slightly confused, I enjoyed it enormously.

I think it only fair to report that I was ready to quit coloring long before Pat was. In fact, I suspect she took up her crayons again after I left for home that evening.

I love the fact that God is a God who encourages relationship not just with himself, but with one another. Jesus modeled that for us in the richness of his relationships with the twelve disciples. We are indeed rich when we have many friends, and I'm thoroughly convinced that God loves us, encourages us, nurtures us, and supports us through other human beings. They can almost become to us Jesus with skin.

May we not become so busy, harried, and overcommitted that we neglect that part of our soul that is fed and sustained by friendship.

Lord Jesus, how grateful I am for other people in your great creation who can cradle my soul and hear my voice in much the same manner in which you cradle my soul and hear me. Thank you for bringing these ambassadors of your love into my world. Amen.

Slippin', Slidin', and Lovin' Every Minute!

> Though he stumble, he will not fall,
> for the LORD upholds him with his hand.
> PSALM 37:24

W hat a fabulous idea! Of course I'd love to ice-skate with you at Rockefeller Center!"

I listened to this enthusiastic declaration from my daughter-in-law, Carla, to my friend Pat the day before Thanksgiving. Pat and I accompanied Jeff and Carla to New York City for the holiday weekend, and what a memorable time we had! It truly was one of those experiences this mother-heart has tucked warmly in her cathedral of memories to be revisited many times as the years go by. (Good grief, Marilyn ... you sound like you're already in a rocker. Get a grip!)

I had no idea Pat had been nursing a desire to ice-skate at Rockefeller Center Thanksgiving morning, and I had no idea Carla even knew how to ice-skate. She happily assured me that she had not skated in twenty-five years, but she was sure that would be no problem. "Some things you just don't forget," she explained. Jeff seemed to feel confident about the plan, but I had visions of Thanksgiving dinner at some New York hospital with Pat and Carla in traction while Jeff and I sat alongside eating pressed cold turkey from a metal tray.

But such was not the case! After renting their skates, loading me with cameras and instructions from Carla to "catch a shot" of her skating backward (something she said she'd never done before but felt might happen "this very day in this very place"), they sailed onto the ice with hundreds of other eager skaters.

I felt enormous exhilaration as I stood rinkside, a part of a scene I'd seen many times on television but never experienced personally. I watched Pat effortlessly glide alongside my lurching daughter-in-law, holding her hand until, within ten minutes, Carla didn't need a hand. I relaxed and started snapping pictures as they waved, bowed, and showed off in various poses meant to depict competence and assurance.

Within a short period of time we at rinkside established a common bond as we shared our experiences about those on the ice. A fifteen-year-old girl stood next to me, lamenting the fact that she had not been able to talk her forty-four-year-old mother out of skating today.

"She's never been on ice skates in her life! Can you believe she's doing this? We come here all the way from Georgia just so she can break her neck in New York City!"

I followed the troubled daughter's gaze and found this adventurous mom slipping and sliding along the ice, grinning from ear to ear. Every now and then she was joined by another woman who grabbed her hand, and together they giggled and groped around the rink. "Who's that?" I asked the anxious teenager. "Oh, that's my aunt; she's as crazy as my mom!"

I soon found myself the official photographer for scores of people on the ice, many of whom were skating for the first time, and almost all of them from places other than New York. One woman from Alabama who was so exhilarated by her unexpected abilities shouted over to me: "Get a shot of this now!" I got a perfect shot of her posterior just seconds before it hit the ice. She was immediately surrounded by gloved hands that pulled her to her feet. Laughing, she called over to me, "Hope you got that one!"

What an incredible spirit of fun and camaraderie there was at that rink! What was the ingredient that so infused the whole experience with irrepressible joy? Was it the exhilarating, yet biting cold? Was it the uniqueness, beauty, and historical dimension of Rockefeller Center? I think it was all of that—but I really believe what surrounded the rink and everyone there was a spirit of caring, kindness, and consistent support. Everyone cheered everyone on. When anyone fell she was immediately helped to her feet and encouraged to continue. We shouted words of praise, clapped in appreciation for every exertion. Even the anxious teenager began to applaud her daredevil mom and "crazy" aunt. There was a tangible sense of kinship—of sisterhood—that seemed to connect us all together.

I think one of the most compelling images in Scripture is found in Psalm 37:23–24. The image of God's extended hand that promises to uphold us provides such sweet security. What better feeling than to be caught before falling by someone who cares about us.

It behooves us all to extend our hand to each sister who slips and slides her way past us in life. She needs us. And before very much time passes, we'll need her.

Heavenly Father, you are a God who upholds us, stabilizes us, and never tires of being there. Create within our hearts a broader, more kindly inclination to extend our hand to whomever you send along this slippery path of life. May we lovingly hold each other up and keep each other from falling. Inspire and enable us to 'be there' for each other as you are there for each of us. Amen.

Did I See That?

Keep on loving each other as brothers.
Do not forget to entertain strangers.
HEBREWS 13:1–2

When Luci left her native Texas to move to California nearly twenty-five years ago, there were numerous little culture shocks she experienced as she attempted to absorb the "peculiar" California customs. One of those peculiarities was that our freeways are often littered with chairs, couch cushions, stray clothing, and various other abandoned treasures. Luci maintained that in Texas we would never see junk like that strewn about the freeways.

We would frequently be zipping (that's when I drove) the freeway only to have our conversation interrupted numerous times with Luci-statements like:

"Can you believe that? Three Tupperware bowls in the middle of the fast lane!" (I don't know how she could know they were Tupperware.)

"How do people lose shoes on the freeway? Does someone simply toss them out? And why only one shoe? I don't think I've seen a pair."

"Oh, Mar, look at that little yellow stuffed gorilla. I wonder why it's yellow. Don't you think it would make more sense if it were brown? I can imagine some little kid feels awful about now. Maybe the mother tossed it out. I don't think I could drive with a yellow gorilla...."

One afternoon we were driving back from Los Angeles at a fairly good clip, and I noticed a green couch off the edge of the freeway not far ahead of us. Luci and I were involved in a pretty heady conversation I didn't want to interrupt, so without announcement I switched lanes and pulled off the freeway several feet away from the couch. With unexpressed but mutual understanding, we both got out of the car, walked to the couch, sat down, and continued our conversation.

You should have seen the whiplash responses of people as they hurtled past. They couldn't believe they had just seen two women chatting animatedly on a discarded couch by the side of the freeway.

We were still laughing as we pulled back into traffic, and Luci said, "You know, Mar, I wouldn't have missed that for the world!"

"Neither would I, Luci. And just think, if we'd been in Texas, we wouldn't have had a place to sit!"

I am of the firm conviction that one of the most winsome as well as healing ways to love each other is to entertain each other. Now I know very few of you would set up shop by the side of the road while cars whizzed past. But there are so many quiet, perhaps more sane ways of loving through entertaining. For instance, the sharing of little anecdotal experiences while at the cleaners, gas station, your office, driving your car pool, etc. Perhaps you could read to each other some odd, peculiar, whimsical, or offbeat thing you saw in a newspaper or magazine. I know one of the reasons I feel so close to the three ladies with whom I share the platform at Joyful Journey conferences is that they entertain me. They teach and encourage me too, but oh, how they amuse me! To me, that's loving.

Incidentally, when these joy offerings are handed out to strangers or observed by strangers, we're fulfilling

Hebrews 13:2. Now maybe the writer of Hebrews was referring to "at home" entertaining . . . but who's to say we can't take it on the road?

Lord Jesus, open my eyes to the little things in life that can entertain and lift not only my spirit but others! May I be aware of this creative way of loving others — even strangers. Amen.

Peanut Butter Yogurt and Raspberry Sauce

"Go and enjoy choice food and sweet drinks,
and send some to those who have nothing prepared."
NEHEMIAH 8:10

One of the most delightfully peculiar experiences that will be forever squirreled away in my store of memories occurred some years ago when we were living in Fullerton, California.

I was indulging in one of my favorite taste treats: peanut butter frozen yogurt slathered in raspberry topping. As I was just dipping my spoon into this incomparable concoction, the door of the shop opened suddenly and a tiny elderly lady burst through it. She scanned the shop for a second and then darted over to my table, pulled out the chair across from me, and sat down.

Before I had quite grasped what was happening, she leaned across the table and whispered, "Is anyone following me?" I looked suspiciously behind her and out into the parking lot from which she had emerged. Then I whispered back, "No, there's no one in sight."

"Good," she said, and with that she slipped out her teeth, snapped open her purse, and dropped the teeth into its depths.

Throughout this unexpected scene my spoon had remained frozen between my dish and my mouth. Galvanized into action by the melting of my yogurt, I put the spoon into my mouth. The little lady fixed her eyes upon my spoon and then upon my dish. I asked if she had ever eaten peanut butter yogurt with raspberry sauce. Without ever looking at me, she said that she had wanted to try it all her life but never had. I calculated that "all her life" was probably some eighty years. I asked her if she'd like me to get her some. Without a moment's hesitation, she said "Yes," but never took her eyes off my yogurt. By the time I returned to our table with her order, she was nearly halfway through my original dish. I found this amusing, especially since she offered no explanation. I started eating what would have been hers, and we slurped along in companionable silence.

Across the street from where we were eating is an establishment for senior citizens that cares for those in fairly good health but in need of watching, as well as those in poor health needing constant attention. I classified my little yogurt companion as an inhabitant of this home. The minute she finished her yogurt, she began rapid preparations to leave. She whisked her teeth out from the environs of her purse, popped them in place, and headed for the door.

Concerned about her crossing the busy intersection alone, I asked if she'd let me accompany her. She was out the door and into the parking lot so fast I almost had to run to keep up with her. As I had surmised, she made her way into the senior citizens' building and scurried down the hall. The only thing she said to me was that she had to hurry or she'd miss lunch.

I stopped at the nurses' station and asked the girl behind the counter if she had noticed the little lady I had come with. She said, "Oh, yes. That's Felisha; she's a real live wire." Then she asked if I happened to be a relative. I told her Felisha and I had just met at the yogurt shop less than an hour ago. The girl's eyes twinkled as she asked, "Did you by any chance buy her a dish of yogurt?" I was a bit startled as I admitted I had. The girl laughed and told me Felisha knew every trick in the book.

I have revisited this memory many times through the years, not only for the deliciously quirky experience it provided, but for the example Felisha provided. Here's a little woman who knew how to get the most out of life . . . even to the point of my paying for it! I'll confess to you right now that Felisha is my model for "at the home" kind of living. When that day comes for me, I intend to join as many strangers as I can who will buy me peanut butter yogurt and raspberry sauce or whatever else they may be eating. According to Nehemiah, that's a scriptural concept!

Dear Lord Jesus, there's so much in life that isn't fun, that hurts and drags us down. Give us the eyes to focus on the stray joys that could so easily slip past us. Help us widen our vision not only to encompass those joy breaks, but to see the ways in which we can bring them to others in whatever stage of life they may be. Amen.

Cookies for Breakfast

When times are good, be happy.
ECCLESIASTES 7:14

As I write this devotional, December 25 is approaching quickly. Not only do I feel the need to leave my desk, get out into the malls, and slug my way through the crowds, I am also finding myself full of floating Christmas thoughts and memories. I love those! I am not advocating sitting about engulfed in "Christmas Past" so that "Christmas Present" is not attended to, but I must admit there are many images that beckon my revisiting. One that has been floating around me much of today (I know it was triggered by some melt-in-your-mouth sugar cookies my neighbor brought over this morning) occurred at 4 A.M. on December 22, 1991.

Ken had been diagnosed with cancer ten months prior to this date and wasn't even supposed to be alive. But not only was he alive, he was doing fairly well. He was gaining some of the hundred pounds he had lost and was regaining strength. We entered this particular Christmas with guarded optimism.

A tiny bit of background before I continue: Ken's mom, Edith Meberg, was probably the best cook I ever experienced, and her Christmas cookies literally defied adequate description. To say they were phenomenal is a verbal start but still not superlative enough to do them jus-

64

tice. A highlight of each Christmas was to open the huge UPS box from Seattle containing her cookie delicacies.

Armed with that information, let's go back now to the morning of December 22, 1991. I am a very light sleeper at best, so I was aware of Ken's restlessness on this particular morning. Aware of mine as well, Ken broke into the silence at 3:50 A.M.: "Marilyn ... I've got a great plan for us for the next couple of hours."

"Really? I assume it doesn't include sleep."

"That's right! The plan for this moment is that I must get up and you are to stay in bed for ten minutes. Then you get up, come down to the living room, and the plan will unfold!"

"Okay, Babe, it shall be as you have said." (My response sounded faintly biblical to my ears—I liked it.)

At 4:00 A.M. I got up and went into the living room, where, in typical Ken style, he had a fire going (gas logs ... no effort), a big pot of tea on the raised hearth, and an arrangement of his mom's cookies on a silver tray with Christmas napkins on the side. He had drawn one of the love seats close to the fire, lit all the Christmas candles, and turned on the tree lights. Christmas music was playing softly in the background.

"Ken Meberg, you have the soul of an artist. What a gorgeous scene!"

With happy enthusiasm, he poured each of us a cup of tea. He then handed me the silver tray of cookies, and with a flourish of his hand said, "Eat as many as you like, Madam."

"You mean I can eat cookies instead of breakfast?"

"Indeed you can, my dear. This is a special occasion."

For several hours we sat in front of the fire slurping tea, munching cookies, and giggling like a couple of naughty children. I don't know when I have enjoyed a tea party more, and I don't know when I have had better company. I was intensely aware of needing and wanting to savor those moments with my husband, and indeed I did. In fact, I still do.

Heavenly Father, you give us many softly beautiful gifts. We thank you for every one of them. Remind us to savor the moments you provide, remembering that each is from you, our Father, given to us in love. Amen.

I Love Presents!

Every good and perfect gift is from above,
coming down from the Father of the heavenly lights.
JAMES 1:17

But, Luci, people would think I am totally out of touch with reality. I mean, there's even the potential of an insanity label with this kind of thinking!"

"Not to worry, Marilyn. Who's going to know? In fact, I'm the only one you've told this to, and I can think of only a very few with whom I would feel compelled to share it."

"You're such a comfort, Luci."

I may as well tell you about my insane thinking since you might be one of those "very few" with whom Luci feels compelled to share.

First, a bit of background. As of this writing, November 19, I have begun to enter into that customary pre-Christmas "I find the holidays especially poignant since Ken died" phase. Ken loved Christmas and was exceedingly creative and generous with gift giving, decorations, cooking, and entertaining. He entered into all phases of the holidays with tremendous enthusiasm and exuberance. It is, of course, only natural for me to miss that wonderful energy he infused into the season. But what is embarrassing for me to admit is that I also really miss the fantastic presents he used to give me. Beginning with my nineteenth birthday, Ken had made an enormous production of gift giving. You've got to admit, that's a lot of years to be spoiled by someone.

Well, I don't know about you, but starting about now I receive daily at least four or five catalogs, many of which carry some very beckoning items that activate my Christmas longings. And yesterday, I was sufficiently activated to come up with the plan I feared might label me as dangerously out of touch with reality.

Here was the plan: There were two catalog offerings that not only appealed to my aesthetic side but my practical side as well. In other words, not only did I want them, I felt I needed them. But how could I justify ordering these two items for myself? Wouldn't that be a bit selfish, possibly self-serving? After all, both of my adult children have needs, and I delight in doing things for them. Shouldn't I just continue in that more selfless mode?

That is when the questionably brilliant idea struck! Why not order them, wrap them, and put them under the tree with a Christmas tag reading, "To Marilyn from Ken." After all, if Ken were still living he would love to get those items for me. But, I thought, that's going to be a bit unsettling for everyone if, as gifts are handed out, there are two "To Marilyn from Ken" presents! My kids are going to think I've really lost it!

As Luci and I were chatting about this yesterday, she enthusiastically endorsed my idea of "To Marilyn from Ken" and even went so far as to tell me in great detail the various gifts she'd purchased for herself, had gift wrapped, and then, in the cozy quiet of her own home, played her favorite music, brewed a flavored coffee, lit the fire, and had her very own party!

I listened with great interest and then said, "Luci, I love hearing about your private parties for just you from you, but have you ever opened gifts from someone who is no longer living?" She stared at me for a moment and then answered softly: "If it were a present from Ken, I'd open it in a heartbeat!"

Occasionally I must remind myself that all gifts are given to me, God's beloved child, with incomparable love and joy. For me to feel guilty about buying myself something is to forget the original Author of that gift. And if I forget that reality, I may then lose sight of his all-encompassing love for me. Everything good and loving in life has its source in God, including all gifts. Actually, if I were to be theologically sound, I'd write on the Christmas tag, "To Marilyn from God." I love that idea!

Dear loving and generous Father, what a comfort it is to call you Father and to be your child. What a privilege to be one upon whom you long to shower your many gifts. May I lift my eyes from the earthliness of life and see again the beauty of your gifts for the enrichment of my soul and spirit. May I keep ever before me that greatest gift of all who, more than 2000 years ago, lay in a manger so I might have not only abundant life, but eternal life as well. Amen.

Savoring the Crown

Children's children are a crown to the aged.
PROVERBS 17:6

Having reached that highly esteemed classification called grandparent, I am not only luxuriating in little Ian's current development, but I'm looking back nostalgically to that of Jeff and Beth's some twenty-five years ago.

It was tremendously important to both Ken and me that I not work outside the home until both children were at least in school. I am thrilled that Beth and Steve are of the same mind. The crucial issues of security and trust are established in the first few years of life, so experiencing less than a warm and trustworthy environment in those beginning stages of living can be devastating to the development of a little psyche.

Nevertheless, there were many times when I felt utterly trapped in my mother-and-child environment. Three days a week Ken would go directly from work to USC for classes. I had no car, was not even within walking distance of a grocery store, and frequently wondered if there was anyone in the world without a pacifier in his mouth. Though I would not have had my life any other way (except to have a car), I occasionally allowed the ever-presentness of parenting to interfere with the savoring of those priceless "kid-comments" that only later did I recognize as precious. Let me give you an example.

I don't know if Jeff was three or four when this happened (I do know he had given up his pacifier, because I could see his entire face). I was attempting to instruct him in how to tie his shoes, which is no small task to explain and no small task to understand. Jeff's spirits were faltering, and I was beginning to tire of my own voice. In fact, I was tiring of not having the opportunity to verbalize anything more lofty than how to tie a shoe.

Yielding to a desire for more high-flown language and tone, I startled Jeff by suddenly launching into a diatribe about England's darkest hour during World War II when the people were close to losing heart, fearing they would soon be defeated by the seemingly invincible forces of the German army. "But," I declared, my tone rising, "there was a lone voice in the midst of all that perilous uncertainty: the voice of one of the greatest statesmen in world history. His name was Winston Churchill. It was he who inspired his people over and over again with the words: 'Never give up — never . . . never . . . never!'"

Noticing Jeff's incredulous little face for the first time since I had gone off into my dramatic rendering, I simply concluded by saying: "So, Jeff, you must never give up — never . . . never . . . never . . . never!"

All that expenditure of energy required a cup of tea, so I retreated into the kitchen, refamiliarizing myself with my life. Upon my return to Jeff's bedroom, teacup in hand, I saw him hunched over his little black tennis shoes muttering resolutely, "Never get up — never . . . never . . . never . . . never!"

As I look back on my years of mothering, my biggest regret is that all too often I did not savor the moments. I was far too concerned with efficiency, tidiness, and order. Now, if I had it to do again, I'd spend as much time as Jeff wanted at the tropical fish store; so what if dinner was late! I'd listen more closely to Beth's endless fiction about a Gertrude Sweatstein and Dr. Bloodworth, whose soap-opera lives she'd made up were undoubtedly reflections of some of Beth's own eleven- and twelve-year-old tensions.

I guess one of God's ways of giving second chances is allowing us to become grandparents. Because you can bet your last gold filling that if little Ian wants my lap, my ear, or my last ounce of energy or creativity, he's going to get it. I wish I had been that consistently generous with his mama.

O God of patience, kindness, gentleness, and graciousness, enable us to be quiet long enough to hear the faltering steps of the little people who attempt to follow us. May they see in us your patience; may they experience from us your kindness; and may our voices reflect your gentle graciousness. Thank you for the privilege of participating in the molding of their characters. May we rise to that highest of callings and savor each blessed moment. Amen.

A Divine Prescription

A cheerful heart is good medicine,
but a crushed spirit dries up the bones.
PROVERBS 17:22

A number of months ago I received a letter from a group of women who had attended the Joyful Journey conference in Atlanta. These dear ladies are in their mid-seventies, widowed, and "kind of take care of each other." Apparently they gather together each week for a Bible study and then go out to lunch. (Sounds like a fabulous double feed to me!)

They loved the Joyful Journey conference and wanted me to know specifically how they had utilized something I had taught. To one of their scheduled times of sharing and study, two of the women came feeling unusually intense arthritic pain, one had a headache that had been hanging on for days, one felt mildly depressed, and the other two said they felt basically indifferent about everything in life ... even lunch. (Red flag right there!)

Realizing this was not going to be an upbeat day for anyone, the unofficial leader of the group and writer of the letter to me suggested to her friends, "Why don't we do that fake laugh Marilyn showed us—you know, the one that put everyone in the auditorium into hysterics?" (In one of my talks I demonstrate how the smallest giggle, when practiced on purpose, can lead to belly laughter within minutes.) Out of desperation, these six decided it certainly couldn't hurt anything, so they started the fake "heh-heh." It sounded so dumb in their ears that they did end up in genuine fits of hearty laughter.

To their amazement, the arthritic pain lessened, the headache became less intense, and the depression and indifference seemed to give way to a feeling of greater well-being. The writer told me that now they begin each of their weekly sessions with prayer, self-induced laughter, and then Bible study. Needless to say, I was touched and pleased by this testimony of God's healing touch from laughter.

When God said a joyful heart (or laughing heart) is good medicine, I believe he was literal in his meaning. The medical world has verified that laughter releases endorphins, God's natural painkillers, which are fifty to one hundred times more powerful than morphine. So when these dear women all experienced a lessening of both physical and emotional discomfort, they were simply taking their God-prescribed medicine.

You are probably aware that the scientific world has been doing a lot of research about the mind-body connection, especially in the realm of laughter. I was fascinated to read an article in the August 11, 1996, London *Times* (Luci sent it to me — I never go anywhere). A researcher named Jonathan Leake has been seeking the answer to why people who laugh live longer. He has discovered how a group of life-enhancing chemicals are triggered by peals of laughter. These hormones are so powerful, they can energize a person's entire immune system and help it ward off diseases, including the common cold or flu.

In the same article it was reported that Arthur Stone, a professor of psychoneural immunology at the State

University of New York who has pioneered research on the effects of laughter, has published a paper outlining the most conclusive evidence yet of a link between laughter and blood levels of immunoglobulin A. (This helps people fight illness by marking invading bacteria and viruses for destruction by white blood cells.)

The search for such organic substances began a decade ago with the discovery of a link between a cheerful outlook and longevity. It was quickly established that melancholic people have higher levels of hormones known as cortisones, which are associated with stress and can damage people's ability to fight disease. Only now is the role of their uplifting counterparts, the cytokines, beginning to be understood.

Don't you love that? The God of the universe has said all along that a joyful heart is good medicine. God has given us a prescription for joy. All we have to do is fill the prescription.

O God in heaven, you love us so completely that you even provide a means by which we can be released from pain and discouragement through laughter. How mind-bogglingly creative! Help us to rise up out of the dark corners of our soul and believe you have indeed provided medicine for joyful healing. May we take at least one dose every day. Amen.

A Firm Foundation

He brought out his people with rejoicing,
his chosen ones with shouts of joy.
PSALM 105:43

Ken Meberg was one of the funniest men I've ever known. In fact, what drew us to each other at the tender ages of nineteen and twenty at Seattle Pacific College was our mutual appreciation of each other's humor.

As our dating relationship grew and became more public, Ken and I were walking across campus one day as Dr. Swanstrom was walking toward us. He was not only one of our favorite professors, but probably near the top of every student's preferred list.

He stopped in front of us and with a warm smile observed, "Well, this looks to be getting serious. Is it?" I smiled demurely as Ken agreed that it certainly was in his mind. With twinkling eyes and a friendly clap on Ken's shoulder, Dr. Swanstrom said, "I just can't imagine the kind of children you two will produce!" Somehow, we felt complimented.

Years later, having produced two children, Ken, Jeff, Beth, and I were about a half block from home one afternoon when Ken simply pulled the car over to the curb, wordlessly opened his door, got out, and began walking in the direction of our home. Within seconds I too got out of the car and began walking. Jeff, taking his cue, got out of the backseat and headed for home. This left our puzzled seven-year-old, Beth, alone in the car. As she watched us walking toward home she finally called out from the back window, "Don't you think I'm too young to drive?"

One evening as we were eating dinner together, Ken, having scooped out his baked potato from its jacket, simply tossed it over his shoulder where it landed in the far corner of the kitchen. Within minutes, Jeff tossed his empty potato skin over his shoulder. Beth, who was somewhere in the vicinity of five years old, looked at me with undisguised pleasure and said, "They're being childish, huh, Mama?"

"They certainly are, Beth."

With a happy smile, she tossed her potato skin over her shoulder and proclaimed, "I'm supposed to be childish!"

These and many more times are wonderful memories I hold in my head as evidence of a somewhat zany but fun lifestyle we practiced in our home.

Because I have so frequently used the themes of joy and humor in my writing and speaking, I'm often asked to give pointers on how to develop a laugh lifestyle. I always find that a difficult question because a laugh lifestyle is so much more than tossing potato skins around the kitchen. It is also so much more than joke books, funny tapes, or humorous movies. They have their place and can certainly provide wonderful times of laughter, but the humor they inspire is external to who we are.

The development of a laugh attitude begins internally. It begins with a foundation that is God-inspired and God-constructed. That foundation gives us security as we stand confidently on the strength of his incomparable love for us. Faith in that solid foundation then leads to personal rest and divine security. Without this internal peace, the laughter inspired by all the zany antics we can think of will ultimately die in the wind, leaving a hollow void waiting to be filled with the next antic or joke.

I guess if I were to reduce all of these words about developing a laugh lifestyle into one sure first step, it would be: Become personally acquainted with the Author and Giver of joy. His name is Jesus.

Lord Jesus, without you our laughter would quickly become hollow and meaninglessness. But you give us reason for being, you give us significance in being, and you fill our being with the awesome assurance that we have been cleansed and forgiven of all sin. Because of the cross, we have been reconciled to you for now and all eternity. Because of that truth we do indeed break forth with rejoicing and shouts of joy. Amen.

Traffic Ballet

But let all who take refuge in you be glad;
let them ever sing for joy.
PSALM 5:11

This morning I was in my kitchen doing the mildly mindless things I do each day between 7 and 8 A.M. Luci had just left, having delivered a grapefruit plucked from her backyard tree only minutes before. (Sometimes I truly think I live in paradise.) I flipped on *Good Morning, America* to see if they knew anything I should and settled into my final cup of tea.

Am I ever glad I did! There was a segment that caused me to whoop with laughter and delight. I couldn't wait to tell you about it . . . in fact, I didn't even finish that cup of tea! I've dashed to my desk instead. Here's what set me off . . .

They interviewed a guy named Tony from Providence, Rhode Island, who is a traffic cop. He described how neither he nor any of the other guys on the traffic detail could bear one duty each of them had for at least an hour a day. They had to stand in the middle of a busy intersection directing traffic, and he said it was so boring and uneventful he could hardly endure it. He decided to try and spice up that dull task with something that would at least entertain himself and make the hour go faster.

He began experimenting with exaggerated hand and arm movements, which led to rhythmically syncopated body swings to go with the movements of his limbs. Finally, after only a few days, he began twirling from left to right, startling drivers with his flourishes of "hurry up," "slow down," or "stop!" That ultimately led to occasionally doing full body spins, which culminated in the splits.

Motorists grew to appreciate his antics so much they honked and clapped until he had so many enthusiastic fans it created traffic jams, which only increased his need to twirl, flourish, and point to get cars moving. To avoid the hazards his accumulation of fans presented, Tony was assigned to different intersections each day so no one knew for sure where he'd be performing.

As this interview was going on we, the viewing audience, were treated to a video of Tony's "intersection ballet." Buses and cars were whizzing past in such proximity to him I wondered if he was ever hit by any of the vehicles. The question was posed to Tony, and he said that he bounced off the side of a moving bus once because he lost his balance during one of his twirls. He said he suffered no bodily harm from the experience but that it did inspire him to do a bit of practicing of his twirls in the basement of his home that night.

What a perfect example Tony is of how to practice a laugh lifestyle. A laugh lifestyle is predicated upon our attitude toward the daily stuff of life. When those tasks seem too dull to endure, figure out a way to make them fun; get creative and entertain yourself. If the stuff of life for you right now is not dull and boring but instead painful and overwhelming, find something in the midst of the pain that makes you smile or giggle anyway. There's always something somewhere ... even if you just have to pretend to laugh until you really do!

You need that joy break, so take at least one every day. Hey, how about twirling and flourishing in your kitchen, grocery store, or office? It works for Tony!

We have joy, dear Father, because we can take refuge in you. You provide our safety, our security, our eternal hope. Because of those loving assurances, enable us to see the joy, feel the joy, and even twirl with joy. Thank you that you are our reason for joy each day. Amen.

How's the Weather?

He turned the desert into pools of water
and the parched ground into flowing springs.
PSALM 107:35

Palm Desert, California, where I live, is for eight and sometimes nine months of the year a paradise. I bask in daily sunshine under blue skies with winter temperatures in the seventies.

Since I am "solar-powered," the presence of the sun is crucial to my sense of well-being. Growing up in the Pacific Northwest, where even summer picnics were frequently rained out, I was thrilled when, in 1961, Ken and I married and headed south for Garden Grove, California.

Ken grew up in Seattle and was far more drizzle-driven than solar-powered. As a result, our first couple of years in the sunny Southland were a bit of a challenge for him. He was surprised to find he missed the gray, sloppy days to which he had become accustomed. (Mark Twain said the mildest winter he ever experienced was the summer he spent in Seattle.)

Even though I too grew up in the Northwest, I never got used to what felt like year-round winter. I didn't realize how much I was oppressed by rain until we moved to Southern California, but my spirits soared the minute we landed in the Los Angeles basin. I'm kind of embarrassed to have my mental health so strongly influenced by the absence of rain and the presence of sun, but it seems to be a fact, whether I'm proud of it or not.

To celebrate our first wedding anniversary, Ken suggested we go to Palm Springs. It was only two hours away, and the hotel rates were reduced because it was the third week of June. Neither of us knew much about Palm Springs except that it sounded like a wonderfully exotic and romantic place to go. That it was located in the Mojave desert didn't strike us as a problem.

As we pulled up to our charming bungalow motel, we noticed the temperature sign on the bank across the street read 117 degrees. That was a bit shocking; we had heard about that kind of temperature but certainly never experienced it.

"This is absurd," Ken snorted, dropping our bags in the middle of the room and falling onto the bed. "Who in his right mind lives in a place like this? Who in his right mind pays to visit a place like this? The air's even too hot to breathe! I'm surprised the streets and sidewalks aren't littered with dead people suffocated by this air!"

"Maybe the city carts off the bodies before they accumulate," I suggested. Since that thought didn't seem to strike Ken as clever, I suggested we stand in the deep end of the pool and breathe through a reed until the sun went down. Making another stab at being clever I said, "Maybe being surrounded by all that water will remind you of Seattle." This time he chuckled and said he would beat me into the pool.

Within a few minutes, we tamed our environment and had a fabulous time. Since we were the only ones in the pool (the others had probably been carted off by the city before we arrived), I sat lipline in the water while Ken took flying leaps off the diving board. I flashed numerical ratings with my fingers and, with shouts of encouragement, told him his dives were rapidly working their way to a perfect ten.

That night we splurged and had a romantic dinner at the Riviera Country Club, played the next day in our still-vacated pool, and then headed home.

"Ken," I sighed contentedly. "I think I've fallen in love with the desert. I'd love to live there some day."

"Are you kidding? That's like saying you'd like to live in an ashtray. No way!"

Ironically, some twenty-three years later, Ken became superintendent of the Desert Sands School District, which encompasses those communities from the city limits of Palm Springs through the city of Indio. An even greater irony is that Ken came to love the desert so much he preferred it to the beach. I do as well, although it took *me* only twenty minutes to decide.

One of the things I find fascinating about God's creation is the way he seems to temper the negative environmental elements with corresponding positive ones. For instance, without the nearly ceaseless rains of the Northwest, no incomparable green scenery would greet the eye from all directions. And the snow that snuggles over Mount Hood, Mount Rainier, and Mount St. Helens would not exist if, at lower elevations, there were no rain. Imprinted forever in my sensory memory is the pungent smell of the rich, damp soil that suggests a mixture of pine needles, grass, and moss. I grew up with that scent in my nostrils, and even today, it's one of my favorite smells.

By the same token, if God had not created water for the desert environment, it would indeed be an ashtray. But because of water, we have luxuriously green golf courses, languidly swaying palm trees, and even streams in the desert. Ringing all this valley lushness is the beauty of the San Jacinto Mountains, which turn into a kaleidoscope of pinks, blues, and lavenders each evening as the sun sets.

God's creative style ensures that something wonderful will offset something less than wonderful. In everything God seems so balanced. I love that about him. I also love that he has placed me in the desert where, during June, July, and August, I can be found at the deep end of the pool breathing through a reed.

Lord Jesus, thank you that you have indeed given abundant life to us, your children. Thank you for the richness and beauty of that life. Grant to me always the will to see that beauty and the spirit to see it as a gift from your loving hand. Amen.

An Unusual Song

Sing joyfully to the LORD.
PSALM 33:1

Prior to a month ago, if anyone had asked if I had an opinion about rain gutters, I would have stared blankly. I have strong political opinions, theological opinions, and even social opinions, but no gutter opinions.

For instance, I have a strong opinion about the color chartreuse. It should be outlawed. Anyone caught wearing it, sitting on it, or using it in any way should be fined heavily and then forced to develop a pleasant working relationship with my computer. Because of the perverse nature of my computer, the latter punishment will prove to be a life sentence.

But an opinion about rain gutters? Well, all that has changed. My conversion experience took place about a month ago.

It began with the warnings about the coming El Niño storms this winter. Since I live in the desert, torrential rains are rare experiences for us. However, given the crabby as well as capricious nature of El Niño, I began to wonder if my little condo shouldn't have rain gutters. The one rain we had last winter did provide a bit of an exit challenge, since the water from the roof above the doorways had nowhere to go but straight down my collar and into my shoes.

When the yellow-page gutter man appeared at my door and asked, "Where do you want your gutters?" I was taken aback. I had assumed the fellow would thread gutters around the roofline of my condo and go home.

"Well," I said falteringly, "I don't want to be rain battered when I come out the door so I guess I want the gutters to prevent that ..."

"So you want them over your two doors?"

I began to realize how greatly I had underestimated the varietal potential of gutters. In a matter of minutes the two of us decided on a custom design that would accommodate my particular ground slope, door positions, and garage location. Never in my life had I considered the various means by which one could divert water down little pipes and spouts that would ultimately spill out somewhere other than down my clothing.

I became so fascinated with the placement of gutters, I couldn't ride bikes with Luci and Patsy without veering off course to sidle up to someone's wall and inspect their gutter configuration. I discovered gutters could dump into shrubbery outside the patio, be positioned with a graceful curve to dump onto the driveway, or even into a neighbor's living room! The potential is limitless.

One configuration on a condo two streets from me greatly troubles me. I don't see how it can work efficiently because, as I peered over the five-foot wall into their back patio, it appeared to me the gutter water wouldn't exit far enough from the slider door. I fear when El Niño comes blustering into our town, these people will have a flooded bedroom.

I would express my concern to them, but they never seem to be home. However, last week I noticed through their dining room window a slightly chartreuse dry-flower arrangement on their coffee table. I've decided I won't make any further efforts to advise them.

All this gutter business highlights a basic tenet for joyful living: the little things in life tend to absorb me, please me, or give me a giggle. I had no idea a world of rain-gutter information was out there waiting to be discovered. But now that I've found it, the subject has provided great pleasure for me.

I must admit, though, the audience for my newfound knowledge seems limited. When Luci, Patsy, and I go bike riding, and I dash off for an inspection along the way, they increase their pedal efforts and disappear around a corner. Neither of them seems to have any desire to develop an opinion about rain gutters. But I guess that's okay. At least their bikes are the right color.

Lord, I love that you are the source of all joy, the inspiration for all song. Thank you that you inspire joyful singing in not only the usual places but also in the unusual. Thank you for new things to sing about and new things to know about. Amen.

Playful People

But Jesus called the children to him and said,
"Let the little children come to me, and do not hinder them,
for the kingdom of God belongs to such as these."
LUKE 18:16

I love playful people! People who aren't too sophisti-cated or too proper to engage in zany antics draw me like a two-year-old is drawn to mud. Ken Meberg was such a person.

One of my favorite exchanges of play with him revolved around an Ajax sticker—you know, the one that covers those little holes in the top of the cleanser can.

That sticker caught my attention one night as I was cleaning the sink. Removing the sticker, I thought it really hadn't seen the last of its usefulness. It was so sturdy and full of "stick-um," it seemed a waste just to toss it into the trash.

Carrying it into the bedroom, I took a guess as to which pair of slacks Ken would wear to work the next day and then placed the sticker on the inside pant leg just low enough so he wouldn't be protected by an undergarment but high enough so any overt hand movement in the direction of the sticker would appear indelicate.

According to my expectations, the next day Ken wore the slacks I had "stickered" but said absolutely nothing about it when he came home. I was dying of curiosity, especially since I knew he was chairing a meeting that required him to stand in front of people most of the day. But I contained myself and didn't ask.

After he had changed his clothes and was in the backyard with our son, Jeff, I tore into the bedroom and checked his slacks. The sticker was gone.

Several weeks later I was speaking at a luncheon and became increasingly aware of a scraping irritation in my right armpit. No amount of subtle movement seemed to bring relief, but to scratch or claw at my underarm seemed ill advised since I was surrounded by rather classy ladies who probably had never yielded to a scratch impulse in their lives. Later, at home, I discovered the strategically placed Ajax sticker in the underarm portion of my silk blouse.

This game went on for weeks with neither of us knowing where or when the sticker would appear. My favorite appearance occurred when a policeman stopped Ken for going through a yellow light that turned red while he was in the intersection. When Ken showed his driver's license to the policeman, he laughed and said, "You really must hate your DMV photo."

"Well, not really..."

"Then why is your face covered up with some sort of sticker?"

Several days later Ken walked into the kitchen holding the limp sticker by one corner and with mock seriousness announced that the sticker had died; it had no more "stick-um." Only then did we settle into a raucous description of our individual experiences with the sticker.

Sometimes I think we responsible adults assume that being playful might be interpreted as being childish, maybe even silly. Admittedly, nothing is more tragic than an adult who fails to gain the maturity and wisdom necessary to live a productive life. But equally tragic are adults who forget how to vent their play instincts.

As in all arenas of successful living, we attempt to work toward a balance. The Danish philosopher Kierkegaard maintains that what we want to remember in living is that "we all possess a childlike quality, but we do not want to be possessed with that quality." To give heedless expression to our childlike impulses is no more desirable than totally to suppress them. The mature person is able to recognize the distinction between the two worlds and choose which world is appropriate for the moment.

Jesus said it's impossible to enter the kingdom unless we become as little children (Mark 10:15). He seemed to place a high premium on that childlike quality. The most profound truth in the universe is that God loves us; yet many miss that truth because of its simplicity. When Jesus said, "I praise you, Father, Lord of heaven and earth, because you have hidden these things from the wise and learned, and revealed them to little children" (Matt. 11:25), he reminds us of how preferable it is at times to be childlike.

Lord, we thank you that you have created each of us with a childlike spirit that is capable of fascination, wonder, and enthusiasm. Teach us to revel in that simplicity and in that freedom, to trust you and to take you at your word. Amen.

Party of Four

Therefore be clear minded and self-controlled.
1 PETER 4:7

Last night I had the fun of buying my grandson Ian his first tricycle. Feeling celebratory, I asked my friend Pat, who had accompanied me on this excursion, if she felt like popping into the pizza place across the parking lot and taking a pizza to my house.

Neither of us was prepared for the inefficiency and confusion that characterized every young person working at the restaurant. After we had waited fifteen minutes to place our order, four different people eventually made an effort to attend to it. With difficulty, one person finally understood that I didn't want two but only one medium pepperoni pizza with thin crust. Another worker asked if it was "for here or to go" while someone else gave me change from my twenty-dollar bill. Yet another worker with sauce on his wrist asked if I'd like to see a menu.

Leaning on the PLEASE WAIT TO BE SEATED sign, I asked Pat if she saw anything on the walls stating "We hire the incompetent." Seeing nothing, we decided they hadn't gotten around to posting their policy yet.

Oddly enough, either through ignorance or compassion about the restaurant policy, people started to pour in the front door and stood about waiting to be seated. Since none of the confused workers felt inclined to host, I thought it only charitable to help out. Grabbing a few menus, I asked the two people at the head of the line to follow me please, and I'd be happy to seat them. Then, after seating a party of four, I noticed Pat had disappeared. I spotted her seating a party of three on the other side of the salad bar. Relieved to have cleared out our waiting space, we settled in to wait for our pizza.

Ten minutes later Pat nudged me. "Marilyn, that party of four you seated over by the window is pointing at you and looking pretty hostile."

"They probably don't know the restaurant policy. Maybe I should go tell them." I walked over to their table hoping to diffuse their anger.

One of the men, in an argumentative tone, asked, "Do you work here?"

"Well, actually, no. I was waiting for my pizza."

"Why did you seat us?"

"Somebody needed to."

The couple sitting at the table next to this crabby foursome, whom I had seated first, were smiling broadly as they listened to this exchange. "We wondered why a hostess was wearing jeans and a sweatshirt," the woman said, "but we were more interested in sitting down than inquiring about your uniform."

At that moment my name was called, and amazingly enough, I was handed one medium pepperoni pizza with thin crust. I walked over to the fun couple and said, "I just paid ten dollars for this pepperoni pizza. I'll sell it to you for twelve."

"Does it have anchovies?"

"If it had anchovies, I'd give it to you!" We laughed, and they thanked me for at least a place to sit and said they would leave in a few more minutes to go down the street to Coco's.

Glancing at the still-glowering party of four, I said, "Your waitress should be with you any day now. Enjoy your meal." I then bolted for the door.

Pat and I giggled all the way home over that crazy interlude. We agreed that the foursome had appeared crabby when they walked in. It wasn't just the lack of service or even my obnoxious behavior that set them off. They undoubtedly lived their lives in a state of perpetual annoyance.

Choosing not to be annoyed by life's annoyances is admittedly difficult at times. I often have to remind myself that I have a choice in how I'm going to respond. I'm not talking about denying my feelings and stuffing them away so they can later come back as a headache or a mystifying body rash. I'm suggesting that once I identify the feeling, I can choose to take control of it instead of its taking control of me. I'm also talking about those pesky annoyances that have the potential to join forces so that by the end of the day they have become one big party of four.

First Peter 4:7 reminds me to be clear minded and self-controlled. If my mind becomes cluttered by the day's annoyances, it's a given that sooner or later I'm going to lose my self-control. If I lose my self-control, for sure I'm going to lose my joy. I hate losing my joy. Fortunately, I have a choice in how I react; just like I have a choice in where *not* to go for pizza.

Thanks for reminding me, Lord, that I don't have to let the small stuff rob me of joy. When I keep my mind centered on who you are and who you are to me, it settles me down and enables me to smile instead of frown. Keep me ever mindful of your loving support through the annoying events of each day. May I reflect who you are instead of who I am. Amen.

On the Run

Wherever I go, I generally have a newsmagazine or a book stuffed in my purse in case I have to wait. Since my personality type rarely waits well, I feel pacified knowing I have something to read if I need it.

Some time ago I was waiting in a dental office I had never been to before. Because I had left home hurriedly, I had neglected to grab any reading material. So I found myself voraciously reading everything on the office walls. I was unsettled by a poster near the door entitled, "Every Morning in Africa." It read,

> *Every morning in Africa a gazelle wakes up,*
> *It knows that it must run faster*
> *Than the fastest lion or it will be killed.*
> *Every morning a lion wakes up, it knows*
> *That it must outrun the slowest gazelle or*
> *It will starve to death.*
> *It doesn't matter whether you are a lion or a gazelle:*
> *When the sun comes up*
> *You had better be running.*

Noting my discomfort with this message, I began one of my interior monologues to figure out what was going on in me. *What troubles you about those words, Marilyn?*

I hate that it's true about the gazelle and the lion. That truth feels so hostile. Why does anyone or anything have to live life under such threat? . . . There's no peace.

That all happened as a result of the Fall in the Garden of Eden. That survivor thing came with the entrance of sin into an otherwise perfect and non-threatening world. It was then that lions started chasing gazelles.

I hate the Fall.

You've mentioned that before, Marilyn. Why do you have to spiritualize everything? You can be a bit of a bore, you know!

My internal arguing came to an abrupt halt when I was invited to enter the "dental chambers." There I learned the gold crown on the bottom left side of my jaw was slightly cracked, which explained why I was experiencing discomfort; it would cost only 1.5 million dollars to have it repaired. I was tempted to bolt out of the office and run like a gazelle, but I was strapped to the chair via my mouth.

Later, when I made my escape, I pondered again that troublesome poster. Not only did I hate the gazelle-lion dynamic, I hated the imperative that I too live under siege and "when the sun comes up you had better be running." Yet the disturbing reality is, at times, we all appear to be running—running literally for our lives. We're running from responsibilities, we're running from hurtful memories, we're running from relationships that require time and discipline to repair, we're running from various fears we think may overtake us, and we're even running from knowledge of ourselves.

Why do we do that? Unfortunately, like the lion and the gazelle, we run because we feel threatened. We run to survive.

In time, the words on that maddening poster led me to some reassuring truths. I don't have to run to survive.

As a matter of fact, I am invited to rest to survive. Matthew 11:28 says, "Come to me, all you who are weary and burdened, and I will give you rest."

I can just see myself running into the outstretched arms of the Savior, who recognizes I am weary from running and offers me a place of refuge from all that threatens to overtake me. He offers me rest, and he assures me of that safe, surviving place with him.

Remember that fantastic verse, Deuteronomy 33:27? "The eternal God is your refuge, and underneath are the everlasting arms. He will drive out your enemy before you, saying, 'Destroy him!'" Now that's a powerhouse verse for any of us feeling besieged by lions. We will find refuge in his arms. We will find rest as he enfolds us to himself. He will even destroy our enemies. What tremendous joy those truths inspire for those of us prone to running.

Having finally made peace with that poster, I found myself again sitting in the dental chair. I said, "You know that poster you have on the wall about the lion and the gazelle? Well, I have some thoughts about—" In midsentence I found myself strapped down, and my mouth filled with nearly everything but the dentist's left shoe.

"Isn't that a great poster," he beamed, continuing to load up my mouth. "I guess you could say that's my basic philosophy for living."

It was then I noticed how hairy his hands, arms, face, and neck were.

Lord, thank you that you are my safe place, my refuge. Thank you for your invitation to retreat there anytime, anywhere. Amen.

Just for Fun

For you make me glad by your deeds, O LORD;
I sing for joy at the works of your hands.
PSALM 92:4

Marilyn, how would you like to go to Antarctica for Christmas?" Luci asked as we made our way to the Palm Springs airport one day last summer.

Swerving the car slightly, I tactfully said, "I can't think of anything more unappealing! Why on earth would I want to go to Antarctica? Why would anyone want to go to Antarctica? Surely you don't want to go to Antarctica . . . do you?"

"It would be a fantastic way to see penguins in their natural habitat," she said cagily, knowing my affinity for penguins.

"But, Luci, I can go to SeaWorld if I need to see penguins! Besides, I'm a grandmother with two grandsons. You can't possibly think I'd miss Christmas with them to have Christmas with penguins. What in the world are you thinking?"

Knowing she had my full attention now, Luci told me she had been reading about a Straits of Magellan cruise that left from Valparaiso, Chile, rounded Cape Horn, and two weeks later concluded in Buenos Aires.

Puzzled, I asked, "How do Antarctica and penguins fit into that?"

"Well, actually, that cruise is full, but this other cruise offers a flight over Antarctica for picture taking as well as a special road trip to Punta Tombo, the site of the largest Magellanic penguin rookery in the world."

Feeling slightly tricked, I nevertheless felt hooked as well. At the benevolent insistence of my kids, who reminded me that this was the year for the in-laws at Christmas, we all had Christmas together at Thanksgiving, and Luci, two other dear friends, and I flew to Chile. We boarded the ship December 13 and headed off for what proved to be an off-the-charts fantastic trip.

The incomparable beauty of Chile astounded me as we moved slowly through the deep fjords, snow- and glacier-capped mountains, and photo-inspiring ice caps. Chilean scenery has to be one of the best-kept secrets in the world. Of course, it could well be that I was finally catching up with what the world has known all along.

By the time we rounded the Horn and headed for Puerto Madryn, I was really hyped. From there we would take a bus trip and travel one hundred miles south to the Magellanic penguin rookery. I'd never heard of this type of penguin (so, what else is new?), but I learned they prefer warm weather, live in little dugouts, and sound like jackasses when they speak. I found all this information compelling, but I wasn't prepared for the utter delight I felt as our bus made its way down to the coastal rookery, carefully threading its way through hundreds of little penguins who didn't care whose parking lot they were on or how big our bus was. They had their own agendas, and we were not on it.

As we exited the bus, we stood literally knee-high in penguins. Some awkwardly headed for the ocean where they fell in, while others milled about appearing to wonder what they should do next.

One particularly friendly penguin seemed to bond with our friend Mary as she leaned down and burbled and cooed in the love language reserved for her two little dogs. The walleyed penguin cocked her head to the far right and then to the far left in an apparent effort to comprehend what Mary was saying.

Then, seemingly bored, the penguin turned to the woman standing by Mary and began an energetic effort to loosen her shoelaces. When the shoelaces would not yield, the penguin pummeled the woman's leg with a succession of flipper slaps that sent us all into hysterics. With that, the penguin harrumphed off. The woman was not hurt, but she sported some memorable bruises the next day.

As we bused our way back to the ship, I felt content and grateful to God for the "works of his hands." To my knowledge, penguins don't serve any useful purpose in life other than to give people like me immense pleasure. Perhaps God put together some things in life for no other reason than that we might "sing for joy at the works of his hands." From the grandeur of the snowcapped glacier peaks to the awkward land inefficiency of penguins, what fun it is simply to "sing for joy" about his creation.

Lord God, thank you for the immense beauty and diversity of your creation. Thank you for the opportunity to revel in it and to know from whom it came. Thank you that it delights your Father heart to give me, your child, joy. Amen.

Whittling in the Woods

That everyone may eat and drink, and find satisfaction
in all his toil—this is the gift of God.
ECCLESIASTES 3:13

I've mentioned before that living in the desert is paradise. That is utterly true for about eight or nine months of the year. However, during June, July, August, and even into September, the word *hades* frequently comes to mind. Triple-digit temperatures that make a person dash from her air-conditioned home to her air-conditioned car characterize those months. But since everything here is of necessity air-conditioned, I don't think that our "I can't get outside" summer environment is any more troublesome than that of places where sleet, snow, and subzero temperatures limit outdoor activity. Every geographical location has its compensations as well as its challenges.

One of those summer compensations for me, an outdoor person, is the Palm Springs aerial tram that travels every twenty minutes to the top of one of our San Jacinto mountains. The mountain station is more than eight thousand feet up; so the minute I step out of the tram, I experience temperatures in the high seventies or low eighties. I also experience incomparable woodsy smells and the sound of tall trees allowing the breezes to glide through their branches. Those breezes caress my wrinkled face and lift my wilted spirits.

With my beach chair and book in hand, I find a spot under one of the many hospitable trees and settle in for a day in the woods. Once again I am in paradise.

One day last August, on a particularly hades-tinged day, I convinced my friend Pat to go up the tram with me. She was a bit hesitant because the vertical ascent up the mountainside in a tram seemingly suspended in midair was a bit daunting. Even though the tram information sheet stated that four tract cables supported the tram, she still wondered if she might not be pushing God's inclination to "keep her from falling."

However, once safely up and settled under the protective cover of a grove of pine trees, Pat understood what I meant about reclaiming paradise. We read our respective books in companionable silence for a while, and then from her purse Pat pulled out a Swiss army knife complete with compass, scissors, screwdriver, and every other conceivable blade known to humankind. She began enthusiastically to whittle the bark off various dead branches strewn about our feet. This activity was accompanied by a tuneless whistling that began to threaten my state of paradise. Casting sidelong glances at her, I noted a look of absorption as well as delight. As she graduated from debarking small dead twigs to larger and larger branches, I finally asked her if she intended to build a little cabin.

Choosing to ignore the mild sarcasm in my question, she said, "Marilyn, I haven't done this since I was a kid; I am having so much fun!"

Up to the point of Pat's whistling I had been engaged in Philip Yancey's fantastic book, *What's So Amazing About Grace?* However, my mild annoyance with the increase of lumberjack sounds gave way to envy as I remembered idly and unskillfully whittling pieces of wood with my dad's jackknife while we waited for the trout to strike our fishing lines.

Laying Yancey facedown in the pine needles, I asked Pat if she needed to take a rest from her labors. If she did, I'd be happy to help her debark her latest dead branch. Smiling knowingly, she handed me her knife. That did it; I was snagged.

I don't quite know how to describe the feeling of utter contentment that came over me as I whittled and debarked away the next thirty minutes while Pat read Yancey. It was nostalgic, peaceful and—amazingly—spiritual. Odd as it may sound, I felt God smiling with me. After all, everything we were experiencing in that haven of wooded coolness was a gift from him: the air, the sounds, the contentment, and even the reflection on our childhoods had their source in God's divine plan.

Scripture says eating, drinking, and even toil are gifts from God. That experience in the woods was a wonderfully good gift. Of course, I went out the next day and bought myself a Swiss army knife. It even has a tiny saw! Now I'm ready for our next whittling time in the woods.

I am surrounded by your many gifts, Lord, and I am grateful. Thank you for those gifts that restore my soul and my body. Thank you that all your gifts are available to me. Thank you that they are given out of the abundance of your Father love. Amen.

Wherever I Am

My purpose is that they may be encouraged
in heart and united in love.
COLOSSIANS 2:2

I love the word *fellowship*. It connotes warm and chatty dinner parties, great walks on the beach, or sitting with someone significant in front of the fire drinking tea and sharing souls.

The Greek word *koinonia* is used in Scripture for our word *fellowship* and is defined as "that which is in common." *The International Dictionary of the Bible* defines *fellowship* as "that heavenly love that fills the hearts of believers one for another and for God. This fellowship is deeper and more satisfying than any mere human love whether social, parental, conjugal, or other." I love that definition, and of course, when I say I love the word *fellowship,* what I really love is the experience of fellowship.

I was so aware of the lack of fellowship potential among other shipboard persons on a South American cruise I took this past Christmas. On the ship were 1,200 people, many of whom I assumed were attempting to escape holiday-induced pain. But it lives within and schlepps along with us even through the Strait of Magellan. I noted at times a poignant sadness that seemed to play across the faces of so many of my fellow passengers.

Many seemed reluctant to socialize, and when they did, they lacked enthusiasm.

In contrast, my three traveling friends, whom I have known and loved for more than twenty years, and I daily experienced with one another the "heavenly love that fills the hearts of believers one for another and for God." Especially rich in fellowship was Christmas Day.

Since it was the first Christmas I hadn't been with my grown children, I assumed I'd be swallowing lumps all day and talking to myself about the value of "letting go" and all that baloney. Instead, the four of us gathered in Luci Swindoll's room, where she had set up a little Christmas tree she had made with children's blocks and decorated with tiny toys she had glued to the blocks. We listened to Christmas music on the portable CD player Mary Graham had stuffed in her luggage, read Scripture, and prayed together. Then we exchanged gifts.

What fabulous Christmas fellowship! It was so deep, so sweet, and so Jesus-centered, it went far beyond the beautiful ship decorations, ship food, and the crew members singing Christmas carols in the ballroom.

However, the ultimate experience of Christian fellowship occurred the day after we disembarked and settled into our hotel rooms in Buenos Aires. Because Luci's brother Orville had pastored for so many years in Buenos Aires, we were eager to attend the church he had planted, watered, and fed. Though he now lives in Miami, he had arranged for the four of us to be taken to the church Sunday morning for the service.

Before we even entered the building, the spirited sounds of singing and clapping met us on the sidewalk, enveloped us, and literally propelled us forward. We were surrounded by radiantly smiling Latin faces singing praises to God with utter abandon. For a number of minutes I could only cry.

Not only was I moved by the powerful presence of the Holy Spirit in that place, but I also realized how rejuvenated I felt to be enveloped by believers. After two weeks on a ship, where the majority of passengers were not spiritually inclined, it felt wonderful to be bathed in the oneness of these dear Christians who hugged and kissed us with such unaffected genuineness. That sweet Sunday will live forever in my memory as I reflect on fellowship that was unhindered by language or cultural barriers.

I am convinced that wherever I am—on a ship in South America, in a church in Buenos Aires, or in my hometown of Palm Desert, Christian fellowship is mandatory for my heart and soul. Nothing can take its place.

How about you? Are you pining for the fellowship that surpasses all others? Get yourself to the nearest Christian and connect. Spend time with fellow believers rejoicing over what you have in Jesus. Sing some songs. Laugh together. Pray for one another. Hug each other. Celebrate the blessed tie that binds you to one another in Christian love.

Thank you, Father, for the God-infused kinship that makes Christian fellowship so fulfilling. Thank you for the indwelling presence of your Spirit that unites our hearts and draws us together. May we reach out to each other, receive each other, love each other, and rest in each other. Thank you for the sweet experience of fellowship that rests on the sure foundation of who you are. Amen.

Eating with Gladness

Go, eat your food with gladness, and drink your wine
with a joyful heart, for it is now that God favors what you do.
ECCLESIASTES 9:7

Finally, one of life's major quandaries has been settled: Frozen turkeys are more flavorful than unfrozen or free-range. For years I have harbored the suspicion that I ought never to buy a frozen turkey if I wanted a truly memorable and tasty turkey dinner. I ought, instead, to choose a fresh, free-range turkey that had lightheartedly poked about the farm without restriction. It only seemed logical that this happy, carefree life would produce a flavorful turkey.

However, this logic was never supported by actual experience. For years, each of our carefully selected free-range turkeys was a bit dry, and the flavor never lived up to our expectations. I figured each year that we had unwittingly chosen a turkey who was a malcontent and simply did not have the motivation or imagination to thrive in its free-range status. That being the case, it might as well have climbed a perch and stayed there until its number was called.

My newfound knowledge about the superiority of frozen turkeys came as a result of findings by the consumer reporter on *Good Morning, America*. With the cooperation of one of the finest cooking schools in New York City, four of the top cooking students were asked to choose which of three roasted turkeys was the most flavorful: the frozen, unfrozen, or free-range. With no background knowledge of the three turkeys, each student chef chose the previously frozen turkey as the most flavorful. Then the TV staff was put to the same test, and they too chose the once-frozen turkey.

Well, that settled it for me! Since Thanksgiving was only a few days away, I snapped off the TV and hurried off to buy a frozen turkey. I stood in front of three enclosed cases and stared at their contents. A number of brand-name turkeys were lying there, but I wasn't familiar with any of the names. I assumed that I should just find the weight I wanted and be off with him or her.

To see the written poundage on each label, I practically had to crawl inside the case and rummage around what felt like a pile of cold boulders. With each movement of the turkeys, I unsettled their configuration. They started to rumble dangerously about. I quickly grabbed a sixteen-pound Jenny O and slammed shut the case, averting a massive avalanche of cascading Jennies heading for the floor.

The directions on Jenny's frozen back instructed me to place her in my refrigerator where she would thaw herself to perfection. I would take it from there on Thanksgiving Day.

With innocent anticipation, I pulled Jenny out of the refrigerator Thanksgiving morning to prepare her for the trip to my oven. She wasn't as stiff as the day we had met, but she certainly wasn't soft and pliable. Soaking her in cold water in the kitchen sink and instructing her to hurry up and thaw, I made a fabulous breakfast of Belgian waffles, bacon, and fruit compote, which would hopefully satisfy the family hunger for more hours than I had originally thought.

Jenny crawled into my oven around eleven o'clock and came out around five in the evening. She was flavorful and moist until I cut more than an inch deep. Then we hit pink meat, which threw me into fits about salmonella potential. We sliced surface pieces all around the body, and later I placed Jenny in a huge stewing pot to cook more thoroughly for future soups and casseroles. (Forget about sandwiches the next day!)

In spite of this mild turkey crisis, my family, some dear friends, and I had a wonderful time together. We laughed, caught up with the events in our respective lives, and even reminisced about the time our golden retriever almost succeeded in pulling a perfectly cooked Thanksgiving turkey off the unattended serving platter. His intention apparently was to sneak out the back door for a private meal.

Coming back to the present and looking into the faces of my kids and friends, I remembered something I knew but often forgot. What makes a gathering meaningful is family and friends. The ingredients for sweet fellowship rest not upon frozen or free-range turkeys but upon a mutuality of love and caring.

Sometimes I forget and allow myself to focus on the externals of a celebration, which, of course, throttles my internal experience of joy. Even if we had been reduced to ordering out for pizza and having Jenny join us in eating the meal, we would have had a great time simply because we were together.

Now, that doesn't mean I won't enter into the turkey debate again; however, I've pretty much decided that next Thanksgiving I'll go back to cooking the malcontents from the free-range farm. At least they're nearly ready for the oven when they come in the door.

Lord, thank you for the blessing of family and friends and loving relatedness. Thank you that your presence in our lives is constant and your love for us unwavering. Thank you for the small giggles about turkeys and that you bid us to eat with a joyful heart simply because you favor us as members of your divine family. Amen.

Anxiety over the Unseen

Do not be anxious about anything.
PHILIPPIANS 4:6

"Here, lady, I got a fork and spoon for ya." I looked into the grubby little face of a five- or six-year-old boy whom I had been eyeballing uneasily before I ever took my place in the cafeteria line. He had been standing guard over the utensils while his oblivious mother piled her plate with macaroni and cheese. He, in turn, handed out silverware to whoever would take it from him. The gesture in itself was innocent enough and actually rather sweet. What troubled me was his fingering each utensil not by the handle but by the part that would ultimately be in my mouth. I have a bit of a "germ-thing," so I was torn between not wanting to hurt his feelings and not wanting to encounter whatever germ culture was represented on his dirty little hands.

As I approached him, I was struck by a flash of brilliance. I bent down and in a confidential whisper told him I didn't need any silver because I always ate with my hands.

His eyes brightened with envy as he said, "You do? Does your mom let you do that, really?"

Jerking my head in Luci's direction, I said, "She doesn't see very well, and usually she can't make out what I'm doing anyway."

He looked over at Luci and then back at me. "Wow, what a great mom!"

As I made my way around the entrée counter, I rehearsed in my mind yet again why I didn't like cafeterias. Even if no well-intentioned but dirty little utensil boy was there, other hygienically questionable people were. And they all touched the serving spoon handles. I noted people often sloshed a bit of sauce on their hands, licked them clean, and then, with their newly slicked fingers, reached for the next serving spoon. How did I know they didn't have trench-mouth germs, which would then take up residence on the spoon handle waiting for me?

Okay, maybe these people didn't have trench mouth, but maybe they had an incontinent parakeet whose cage they had tidied up just prior to coming to the cafeteria. Or what about the guy wearing the Digby O'Dell Mortuary shirt who was sifting through the fried chicken container in search of drumsticks? Was it just my imagination that those drumsticks seemed to stiffen at his touch?

"How long have you had this germ thing?" Luci asked after questioning why I was eating my entire meal with an oversized spoon I had found in an obscure container hidden slightly behind the soft ice-cream machine.

"Since the sixth grade."

"What happened in the sixth grade?"

"Our science teacher had us all touch some specially treated sponge, and overnight it grew bacteria cultures that we watched develop into various colorful and horrifying configurations. I've never been the same since."

Luci slowly put down her fork and studied it for a second. Then, with renewed enthusiasm, she announced, "If those germs haven't gotten me by this time in my life, I don't think they ever will!"

Her healthy response reminded me that for me to fear the unseen and worry about its potential to do harm throttles my joy. Of course one should observe hygienic health practices, but if carried to an extreme, they can lead to wrestling with a too-large spoon in a cafeteria with plenty of right-sized forks. Not only that, but also God has created within each of us a miraculously effective immune system designed to ward off the consequences of grubby fingers.

Fortified by those encouraging thoughts, I headed back to the utensil containers for a fork. Of course, I must admit this brave action was encouraged by noting that the little grunge-fellow hadn't been near the utensil counter for at least ten minutes—he was finishing his mother's macaroni.

Lord, so many experiences in life make us anxious and steal our joy. Help us to keep everything in perspective and to rest in your provision. Thank you for your patience and love during those times when our thinking gets out of whack. Thank you that you bring us back to that centered place where we can be "anxious about nothing." Amen.

Freedom for Nothing

We have been released from the law
so that we serve in the new way of the Spirit,
and not in the old way of the written code.
ROMANS 7:6

One of my favorite activities in life is reading. As a child raised in rural communities with few libraries, I was thrilled when the bookmobile rolled into my area every other week. With my books strapped to the back carrier of my bike, I would eagerly pedal a little more than a mile to where the bookmobile was parked at the end of Williams Road. Happily fortified with new summer reading selections, I'd pedal back home, clamber up the makeshift ladder to my tree house, and settle in with my new book friends.

As an adult, most of my reading has been what I would call "meaningful." You know, life-enhancing, spirit-enlarging, or mind-expanding reading. But about a month ago, I experienced a throwback to the days of the bookmobile. Because of an unexpected and rather lengthy delay in a return flight from Dallas to Palm Springs, I wandered into an airport bookstore with the intention of picking up a pleasant "no-brainer," since I had finished reading everything I'd brought with me.

I stumbled onto a paperback that looked pleasant and would allow me to keep my pen in my purse. (Rarely can

I read without a pen in hand because so often a word, sentence, or paragraph will be so terrific I have to underline it, make notes about it, or even talk back to the author in the margins.) This book appeared to be nonprovocative but also nonboring, a great combination for the moment.

Several hours later, as we lurched onto the windswept runway in Palm Springs, I finished the book and smiled happily. "Marilyn," I said, "when was the last time you settled in for a mindlessly pleasant read? Why don't you do that more often? How come you feel you're wasting time if you're not reading Philip Yancey, Eugene Peterson, or Henri Nouwen? (Just for starters. . .) What is driving you continually to be productive? Have you forgotten those lazy afternoons in your tree house when you just kicked back and floated where your book-inspired imagination took you?"

With an abruptness that matched the plane's grinding halt at the gate, it hit me that I had settled into some legalistic thinking about my reading habits. Unless my reading contributed to my spiritual or intellectual growth, I didn't take the time. I'd gotten a bit out of balance, and I suspected I'd been thinking that way for some time. What a loss!

I do gain much pleasure from reading meaningful material; it is not a grind or a chore. But not to allow myself any other kind of reading was unbalanced and a bit narrow.

In an effort to put myself back in balance, I've decided I will do enjoyable but mindless reading on airplanes only. This decision, however, has not proven to be problem free. On my last flight, I found myself uncomfortable reading *Uppity Women of Ancient Times* instead of *Healing Meditation for Life* because the flight attendant had attended one of our Joyful Journey conferences and benefited from it. I found myself camouflaging my book between the pages of *Today's Christian Woman* in case she should see my book title and think me shallow. At least I had the good sense to leave *Do Penguins Have Knees?* in my briefcase.

Perhaps some of you, like me, are missing out on recreational activity that has no purpose other than to give a needed respite from our task-oriented lives. Wouldn't it be fun occasionally to produce nothing, accomplish nothing, and contribute to nothing? Maybe that means reading a book that doesn't require a pen, or maybe it's a meander through the mall or a stroll (not a jog) through the park. The possibilities for nothing are endless.

Lord Jesus, it is so liberating to know you love me for who I am and not for what I do. I have been set free from the laws that require me to perform to be acceptable to you. Now, because of Jesus, I am made perfect in spite of my imperfection. Teach me to rest and enjoy the life and world you have placed me in. Restore my joy as I luxuriate in my freedom from the "old way of the written code." Amen.

Let's Face It

I can do everything through him who gives me strength.
PHILIPPIANS 4:13

When Ken and I first moved to Laguna Beach, California, I was excited about walking the beach each morning as my exercise routine. I saw it as an exhilarating way to stay fit, to talk to the Lord, and to revel in my surroundings.

One morning, about three weeks into my daily reveling, I was making my way down to Main Beach when I noticed over my right shoulder what looked like a Doberman trotting some distance behind me. I had no reason to be alarmed, but I was the only one on the beach, and the dog was not on a leash. That made me a tad nervous. After all, Dobermans are known to be fierce guard dogs. Maybe he felt the need to fiercely guard the beach. I picked up my pace. So did he!

Looking edgily over my shoulder, I noticed the dog was gaining on me. He wasn't running, but he was doing what I'd call a fast trot. I, too, broke into a fast trot. That seemed to encourage him to increase his speed, so I increased mine. Within a short time, I was moving at a full-out run. So was he. I began to huff and puff. As the dog continued to gain on me, I envisioned newspaper headlines, "Middle-Aged Woman with Nostrils Full of Sand Found Facedown, Dead from a Massive Heart

Attack." Or "Woman's Shredded Remains Found Scattered along the Sands of Laguna Beach, Unidentified Dog Sitting Close By with Blue Sweatshirt Threads Dangling from Mouth."

I didn't like either of those headlines, yet I knew within moments he would be upon me. So I abruptly stopped running and turned to face him. He was delighted. He came bounding up to me, tail wagging and obviously eager to be petted. I stroked his face and neck and then dropped onto the sand with exhaustion and relief. To his obvious delight I scratched his ears and told him what a fright he had given me. He didn't seem to comprehend anything other than that he had made a new friend. Together then, we ultimately arrived at Main Beach, with his stopping repeatedly to wait for me.

I have metaphorically applied that story to my life many times. For instance, I have envisioned certain fears that I would try to keep ahead of, only to find that when I stopped and faced them, there really was nothing to fear after all. What I needed to do was quit trying to avoid them and face them instead.

After my husband died, I didn't think I could handle money matters like taxes, interest rates, and investments. After all, I have a number phobia. No one with a number phobia can figure out and keep track of stuff more complex than the price of broccoli, cauliflower, and grapefruit. I had no choice but to turn and face that fear. I would still rather deal with investments like broccoli, cauliflower, and grapefruit, but I have learned it won't leave me dead on the beach to read a tax form.

Dashing ahead of the Dobermans of life leaves me breathless and scared. Facing them with a prayer on my lips and faith in my heart allows me not only to trust God more but also to experience victory that comes from no one but him. Actually, that is a rather exhilarating way to stay fit.

Father, thank you that my ability to face down my inadequacies and fears comes from your promise that I can do everything through you. Thank you for the exhilaration of seeing and feeling your strength working in me. I am grateful. Amen.

Who Do You Be?

Before I formed you in the womb I knew you,
before you were born I set you apart;
I appointed you as a prophet to the nations.

JEREMIAH 1:5

My grandson Ian bequeathed upon me a most unusual name when he was about fifteen months old. The name is "Maungya." We are unaware of its origins other than that it sprung from this little fellow's fertile mind.

I love the name. Lots of Grandmas, Grannys, and Nanas populate the world, but to my knowledge, there are no Maungyas. That name sets me apart, makes me unique. He calls his daddy's mother "Nana" and my daughter Beth's biological mother "Nana Sherry," but my designation is like no other.

During my last visit, the two of us were playing in his sandbox. I was sifting the sand through a sieve in an effort to eliminate the ground cover bark that had managed to get into the mix and annoyed me slightly.

My intensity for this task was intruded upon by an unexpected question from Ian. "Maungya, who do you be?"

Noting the seriousness of his big blue eyes, I felt compelled to answer the question seriously but found myself at a loss for words. Quoting Ephesians 1:4, that I was one chosen before the foundation of the world to "be," seemed a bit theological for the moment. Telling him that Jeremiah 1:5 says I was known even in the womb and designed to "be" also seemed a bit heavy.

I opted for saying, "Maungya is your grandma."

"I know," he said with slight irritation.

"And," I continued, realizing I hadn't answered well yet, "God made her to love you really, really big just like God loves Ian really, really big."

At this, Ian discontinued putting back in the sandbox the bark that I had managed to sift out and stared off into space. Quietly, he repeated, "Maungya loves Ian really, really big." After a few more seconds he said, "God loves Ian really, really big."

Seemingly satisfied, he said, "Yeah, yup," an expression he used to indicate agreement as well as finality on whatever subject is being discussed.

We then resumed our futile take-the-bark-out, put-the-bark-back activity with renewed camaraderie.

I, of course, have pondered this little exchange ever since. The questions of "Who do you be? Who do I be?" are foundational to all of us. We want and need to know who we are. I'm just a bit stunned that Ian is giving it thought already.

The question is asked in Lewis Carroll's *Alice in Wonderland*, "Who in the world am I? Ah, that's the great puzzle!" But, of course, for the believer, there need not be a puzzle. Referring back to Jeremiah 1:5, I learn who "I be."

To begin with, I was in God's mind before I was ever in the womb of my mother. The phrase "Before I formed you in the womb I knew you" is mind-boggling. Specific attention, thought, and planning about me took place before God actually formed me in the womb. That implies I am much more than a cozy encounter between my parents nine months before I was born. No matter the circumstances surrounding my conception, I am a planned event.

Not only am I a planned event, I was "set apart," called or given to be a "prophet to the nations." I, like Jeremiah, have a specific task to do for God. We all have a specific task to do for God, and it was planned in his head before we were ever formed in the womb. That is an incredible truth!

Not only is my identity and calling known, but also Isaiah 43:1 says, "I have called you by name, you are mine" (RSV). I can't imagine God calling me "Maungya," but I do know that like that name, he considers me unique and set apart, and he calls me his own. I can't wait to tell all this to Ian in a few more years. I suppose by then there will be only bark in the sandbox.

Lord Jesus, the knowledge that each of us is a unique, made-to-order creation whom you love, whom you call by name, and for whom you have a plan is security-producing. May we sink into that cushion of joyful peace and never forget "whose we be." Amen.

Daddy

"I will be a Father to you, and you will be
my sons and daughters," says the Lord Almighty.
2 CORINTHIANS 6:18

Certain animals always make me giggle. The more
peculiar they look, the more awkwardly they move,
the more off-the-wall their habits, the more they amuse
me. This summer I had occasion to be in London and was
contentedly perusing the *London Times* one morning
while drinking a cup of brisk English tea. As I flipped
over to page four, to my utter delight the newspaper
showed a huge picture of a baby ostrich. This baby was in
the act of running as fast as its spindly little legs would
carry him. Ostriches rank among the highest giggle-
producers for me, and so I dove into the story with high
expectations.

Instead of finding the story funny, I found it charm-
ingly poignant. A gentleman who owns the zoo in
Welland, Worcestershire, faced a dilemma. He needed a
father ostrich for four recently hatched babies. As soon
as chicks are hatched in the wild, the father runs off at
top speed followed by his brood. This develops the leg
muscles, which ultimately enable the ostrich to run up
to forty miles per hour.

However, these little chicks were not born in the wild
but in the zoo. So the zoo's owner was advertising for vol-
unteers to impersonate a male ostrich for two hours a

day. The volunteer must be able to run twenty miles per hour and flap his arms like wings at the same time. The owner of the zoo said the person needed to be fit because, if you stop running, the baby sits down.

"A top athlete would be ideal for this job," the gentleman said, "but any fit individual who doesn't mind flapping and running at the same time would be great. The chicks think you're their father. They have good eyesight, but they aren't very clever."

I was amused at the thought of volunteering to impersonate a male ostrich, but I found myself more caught up with the need of the babies to have a father who would teach them what they must know to survive in the world.

In contrast to the gentle poignancy of that story is the account I read last week about juvenile delinquent elephants who are killing rhinos in Pilanesberg National Park in northwestern South Africa by kneeling on them and then goring them. The youthful elephants have no motive for killing other than what appears to be the pleasure of it.

Game wardens and animal behavior experts have a theory, and while they stress that it's speculative, the idea is arresting. The troublemaker elephants are all orphans, taken as calves from their parents during cutting operations in the Kruger National Park. The babies were relocated to establish elephant populations in parks and private reserves throughout South Africa.

Most of the relocated calves were males and were raised with no exposure to adult elephants or the hierarchical social structure that defines elephant life. The long-term effect of this isolation appears to be a generation of juvenile delinquents. Under normal circumstances a dominant older male elephant keeps young bulls in line. For the newly relocated elephants, no such role models exist. Early next year, a few forty-year-old bull elephants will be moved to Pilanesberg to help calm things down.

The parallel between the fatherless elephants in need of a strong male role model and our own human societal structure is striking. We know juvenile crime is highest among those who come from broken homes without fathers.

Isn't it interesting that the divine imprint for order in our world is evidenced in all of creation, both animal and human? God created the male to perform a God-inspired role. When that role is disrupted, abandoned, or aborted, disorder and chaos often result. Of course at times a father's absence doesn't bring disorder as much as it brings a deep sense of loss in male modeling.

Ken's father died when Ken was twelve, and he retained wonderful memories of his dad's commitment to Christ and family. Even so, there was a hole in Ken's soul that could never be filled. He wanted and needed a dad to guide him through his teenage years, the choosing of a career, and the development of his theology of living. In spite of a loving mother, at times he needed a dad.

One of the most touching Scriptures is Galatians 4:6, in which God says to us, "Because you are sons, God sent the Spirit of his Son into our hearts, the Spirit who calls out 'Abba, Father.'" The Hebrew word *abba* means "daddy." We are reminded that we are never totally fatherless, and in times of quiet despair, we can cry out a prayer like this:

Daddy, oh, Daddy, comfort me, hold me. I so need your touch. I so need your tender presence. Be with me, dear Daddy. Let me rest in you, relax in you, and find peace in you. Amen.

Rats Giggle

If it is encouraging, let him encourage; if it is contributing
to the needs of others, let him give generously.
ROMANS 12:8

This morning I read this headline in the newspaper:
"Rats Giggle, Tests Find." A researcher at Bowling
Green State University found that rats are not only playful, but they also love to be tickled. Apparently, scientists
have known that about rats for some time, but psychobi-
ologist Jaak Pankseep is doing a study on rats that
attempts to track the biological origins of joy.

What I found fascinating was Jaak's description of
how to make a rat giggle. He says, "It's quite easy. Rats
are small, of course, but it's really no different than using
your fingertips as if you were tickling a child. You get the
most laughter at the nape of the neck."*

In case you, like I, wondered how in the world one
would know if a rat is laughing, their sounds are recorded
by using "bat detectors," sophisticated instruments that
register high-pitched sounds humans cannot hear. "When
a bunch of rats are all tickled at the same time," Pankseep
says, "it sounds like a children's playground at recess."

Of all creatures on the earth, in my mind rats would
be the least likely candidates to take giggle breaks. I have

Los Angeles Times, May 4, 1998, Section A.

found myself smiling about that fact all day. The article has also caused me to spin off on a reverie concerning "least likely" humans I have either known or briefly encountered whom I wondered if a smile, giggle, or laugh ever escaped their frozen lips.

Eighty-year-old Mrs. Davidson falls into the frozen-lip category. Yet, as a child, I found her fascinating. A good part of my fascination was undoubtedly that she would occasionally shout out disagreements during my father's preaching. I, on the other hand, wasn't even allowed to interrupt during second-grade reading group, much less Dad's sermons. I was tremendously envious of all she got away with.

Since she lived within walking distance of our parsonage, I loved dropping in on her. She never seemed particularly glad to see me; instead, she appeared indifferent to my visits. She had an acre of land on which she housed a number of chickens, a goat named Bert, and a cow also named Bert. (I never thought to question the duplication of names or the appropriateness of a cow's having such a moniker.) Mrs. Davidson was always puttering around outside doing various little chores, and I trailed along behind her chatting and trying in vain to engage her in some way.

One night at supper my parents quizzed me about why I liked visiting Mrs. Davidson. I think they were concerned that she might find me a nuisance or that she might hurt my feelings. I told my parents I liked her animals and loved the smell of her few bales of alfalfa, but more than that, I wanted to make her laugh. Both parents put down their forks and looked kindly at me.

"Honey," my father said, "I've never even seen Mrs. Davidson smile, much less laugh."

One of the things we did as a small family of three was make various bets. Dad always was betting my mother about some academic subject he was sure he was right about, only to find he was totally wrong. That never seemed to squelch his enthusiasm, however, and the bets continued as long as they lived.

Thinking I might get in on the betting game, I said to my parents, "I'll bet I can get Mrs. Davidson to laugh before I'm in the third grade!" Rising to the challenge, they agreed and said they hoped I would win the bet. Mom asked what kind of payoff I wanted.

"French toast for breakfast every Saturday morning for six weeks," I said without hesitation.

For at least a month I tried every conceivable thing I could think of to make Mrs. Davidson laugh. I told her jokes; I told her all the bad things Lester Courtney did in school; I even did acrobatics for her. No response.

Then one day, as I was heading up the path toward her messy property, I was attempting to perfect my imitation of how Mr. Brownell walked. Mr. Brownell had caught his leg in a threshing machine at some point in his life, and the accident resulted in the most memorable walk I'd ever seen. Whenever his weight landed on his bad leg, his whole body would veer dangerously out of balance. But somehow the flapping of his arms caused him to catapult in the opposite direction until everything appeared to be back in order. His head moved in perfect rhythm to all this disjointedness. It was quite a feat.

I had been working on this imitation for some time purely for my own sense of accomplishment. My efforts were interrupted by the sound of what could be likened to a donkey's braying. It grew louder and louder until finally I located where the noise was coming from. Mrs. Davidson was leaning against the side of her chicken house, laughing. She laughed so long, so loud, and so hard it made me a little nervous. It seemed to me making that much noise could kill a person.

"Well, Mr. Brownell," she finally gasped, "how nice of you to visit me," and then she went into another braying episode.

When I triumphantly announced to my parents that I had won the bet, they were concerned that the laughter had come at the expense of another's misfortune. I explained that I had been working on the walk for weeks but never intended it to be used for Mrs. Davidson. In fact, I further explained, I had no idea she saw me until I heard her laugh. Apparently convinced that my heart was not cruel, I was rewarded with French toast every Saturday for six weeks.

I still find myself wanting to make people smile or laugh. It's a little game I play with myself when experiencing a gloomy waitress, bank teller, store clerk, or any other frozen-lipped personage. Scripture states that we are to be encouragers and to meet others' needs. What a fun way to take that verse seriously and make an effort to meet the "joy needs" of those around us. It sure beats tickling rats.

Lord, as you increase our joy, may we make an effort to spread that joy around us in your name. Amen.

What a Guy

As a bridegroom rejoices over his bride,
so will your God rejoice over you.
ISAIAH 62:5

Eight years ago today, as I write this devotional, Ken Meberg burst through the portals of heaven looking, I'm sure, for something that needed to be organized. He was a wonderfully competent guy who kept me aware of time and place.

I knew what time it was and where I was; I just didn't think about it much. To this day, I live in the moment and frequently find it amazing one ought to be aware of things that aren't in the moment. Understandably, that characteristic was an occasional burden to my long-suffering husband, but his patience and creativity ultimately set me on a more balanced track.

When we were first married, my car would occasionally run out of gas. I knew intellectually that a car runs on fuel that must be replenished from time to time. But on the other hand, once the car had been gassed up, I was surprised it wouldn't stay full. The same inefficient law of nature extended to groceries. How on earth could we be out of Tabasco sauce; I bought some once.

One of the greatest challenges I contributed to Ken's life was during the third year of our marriage. We decided to obtain a credit card to help us in time of need (which happened to be at the end of each month). I found the card a wonderfully handy benefactor and began to avail myself of its generosity. My usual illogic applied to this card. I didn't seem to remember that what was purchased yesterday needed to be paid for today. Mercy, other things are going on right now.

Ken had mentioned the overuse of the card to me several times, and I had listened conscientiously at the moment. But, of course, that moment soon became past tense and . . . well, you know.

The doorbell rang one morning as one-year-old Jeff was dazzling me with his ability to lurch about the room without holding onto anything. (This action is commonly called "walking," but Jeff's movements were more accurately described as "lurching.") I opened the door to a stern-looking gentleman who asked if my name was Marilyn Meberg. After I owned up to that fact, he asked if he could please see my Bank of America card. That struck me as an odd request, but I innocently pulled it from my wallet, which was in proximity to the door. He asked if he could examine it. I mindlessly handed it to him. (Do not try this in your own home; only the professionally mindless are qualified to accomplish this feat.)

With a dramatic flourish, he pulled from his pocket a small pair of scissors and sliced the card in two. I stared at him in disbelief as he handed the two card pieces back to me. Turning on his heel, he said, "That's what happens to card abusers!"

I stood rooted to the spot long after he disappeared down my walkway. Slowly, the scenario began to make sense. I started to grin, giggle, and finally guffaw. "Ken Meberg, you're good."

That evening, after Jeff had been bedded down, I joined Ken in the living room to read the paper. "Hey,

Babe," I said to the newspaper that shielded his face from me. "I had a fun experience today."

"Really," he said tonelessly, without lowering the paper.

"Yeah, a guy came to the front door and, based solely on my good credit, offered me a MasterCard with a ten-thousand-dollar line of credit!"

Silence.

"Well, what do you think?"

Lowering his paper, Ken said with mischievous eyes, "That didn't happen."

"Well, how do you know?"

"'Cause that's not what I paid the guy to do!"

"You character! You really hired some guy with a suit and scissors to come to the front door and discipline me?"

"Yup," he said, picking up the paper.

"Where on earth did you find him?"

"I'm not telling; I might need him again!"

I miss Ken. I've wondered if he's keeping track of me from heaven and knows that I pay the bills, manage my finances, never run out of Tabasco sauce (which is easy because I don't use it), and keep gas in the car. Not only that, I have one credit card that I pay off at the end of each month. I think he would be proud of me. He contributed enormously to "growing me up," and I'm grateful.

In addition to preventing my life from having its edges tinged with chaos, Ken made me laugh. I never knew for sure what he was going to do or say, but at least once a day he would whiplash me with giggle inspirations. Like the time he gave me a birthday present in a huge box that progressed down to a tiny box. In the tiny box was a little gold charm for my bracelet. Guess what it was? A small pair of scissors. What a guy!

I wish the verse I selected for this devotional read, "As a bride rejoices over her bridegroom," because that's how

I still feel about Ken. Our rejoicing over each other was a sweet gift. But God's rejoicing over us is even sweeter. We come into this relationship with all the flaws of a young bride but also with all the wonder, trust, and love. God, in turn, helps us to "grow up" in him. What a God!

Lord, thank you for love and the richness it provides. Thank you for creating within us the capacity to express that love. Thank you that you model for us the kind of love that rejoices over one another and that your love never dies. Amen.

A Joyful People

You will go out in joy and be led forth in peace.
ISAIAH 55:12

Remember tight-lipped, eighty-year-old Mrs. David-son? She never appreciated my dad's easy laugh or his use of humor in the pulpit. She was given to sponta-neous interruptions during many of his sermons. A color-ful, unpredictable, and off-center little woman, her behavior and tongue couldn't be tamed. If Dad said some-thing she didn't agree with, she would simply shout out, "Pastor, that's a bunch of hooey!"

He took it in stride and went on with his sermon. The people in our small congregation were used to her and didn't seem bothered. I was the one who eagerly antici-pated her various outbursts, and my seven-year-old soul was deeply disappointed if a service didn't include Mrs. Davidson.

One Sunday, Mrs. Davidson was feeling especially vocal. Dad was barely into his sermon when she shouted, "Pastor, no one can laugh as much as you do and call him-self a Christian."

Smiling, Dad pushed his sermon notes aside and spoke the rest of the hour about why joy needs to per-meate every aspect of the Christian's life. Mrs. Davidson was uninspired and unmoved. The congregation, how-ever, clapped heartily when he concluded.

Though I now recognize that Mrs. Davidson's behavior was probably rooted in dementia of some sort, her viewpoint has historical precedent. In the "Ordinance, Second Council of Constance," written in 1418, it says: "If any cleric or monk speaks jocular words such as provoke laughter, let him be anathema." (I had to look up the word *anathema*; it means "a formal ecclesiastical ban, curse, or excommunication." That's pretty serious.) In the fourteenth century, my father would have been banned as well as cursed for his use of humor in the pulpit.

Charles Baudelaire, an eighteenth-century French poet, said, "Laughter is one of the most frequent symptoms of madness."

Isn't it amazing that laughter could have had such bad press for so many centuries? I'm heartened by the words of the twentieth-century C. S. Lewis, who wrote in *Reflections on the Psalms,* "A little comic relief in a discussion does no harm however serious the topic may be. In my own experience the funniest things have occurred in the gravest and most sincere conversations." My kind of man!

In contrast to the leaders of the fourteenth-century Second Council of Constance, Scripture lauds joy as a fruit of the Spirit. In fact, Acts 13:52 states, "The disciples were filled with joy and with the Holy Spirit." It sounds as if both joy and the filling of the Spirit happened at the same time; joy must be important in God's eyes. Galatians 5:25 says, "Since we live by the Spirit, let us keep in step with the Spirit." Does that mean Christians who don't evidence joy aren't keeping in step with the Spirit?

Now, I realize joy and laughter aren't the same. A person can feel joy and not be laughing. But Acts 2:28 seems to encourage more than just interior joy. "Thou hast made known to me the ways of life; thou shalt make me full of joy with thy countenance" (KJV).

I love a smiling countenance; I love even more a laughing countenance. Something is so winsome in the sound and look of laughter. It makes me want to join in even if I'm not sure what the laughter is about. It just sounds fun, and sometimes that's good enough!

I wonder if we Christians may need to pay more attention to our countenance. I can't think of a more compelling witness of my faith in God than to have my joy bubble over into laughter.

Incidentally, Mrs. Davidson continued her mirthless interruptions until the day she died at the age of eighty-six. She was hammering the last few boards onto her new chicken house when she dropped dead from a heart attack. Dad was the one who discovered her, still clutching her hammer. And while the congregation didn't miss her joyless editorials, knowing what she had missed in life left everyone a little bit sad.

Lord, don't let me waste time being negative or joyless. May I seek to show evidence of the Holy Spirit's presence in my life, and may I give witness to those around me that God's people are joyful people. Amen.

Storm Warning

To all who received him, to those who believed in his name,
he gave the right to become children of God.

JOHN 1:12

Vacate your room immediately and head for the stair-well. Proceed to the main ballroom on the first floor. This is not a drill. Vacate your room immediately." Those of us who travel together for the Women of Faith conferences had been in our Nashville hotel rooms for only fif-teen minutes when this frenetic voice came crackling over the intercom.

Prior to this message, I was looking out my twenty-fourth-story window, commenting that the sky had become ominously dark. Peering over my shoulder, Mary Graham had noted lightning dancing crookedly down the street below us. Luci, ever the shutterbug, had shouted, "I have to get my camera. This is amazing!" Instinctively, we all had drawn back from the window as we became aware of the building's swaying motion.

"Good grief," I had said intelligently. "Is this a tor-nado? I've never been in a tornado. Scores of earth-quakes, but never a tornado!" No one was interested.

My storm suspicions were then confirmed not only by the voice on the intercom but also by the debris flying past the window. When a portion of the metal façade from the front of the hotel went hurtling by, we decided to hotfoot it to the stairwell. As we staggered by Luci's room (the motion had reduced us to unseaworthy sailors), Luci was faced with the dilemma of blowing away for the sake of a memorable photo or joining us in the stairwell. Deciding on the stairwell, we all began the trek down twenty-four flights.

"Mercy, is this only the fourteenth floor?" I gasped as everyone went huffing past me—everyone except Luci. We decided we weren't interested in making it to the ballroom anyway. As far as I was concerned, sitting cross-legged in the corner of the stairwell had become increasingly attractive. Luci thought anything was more attractive than hiking down ten more flights; so she voted for joining me in the corner. The lady in front of me from New Jersey liked the idea as well. The problem was that there really wasn't a corner; if we just sat down, we would be an obstruction to those determined to reach the ballroom. Reluctantly, the lady from New Jersey, Luci, and I rejoined the heavy breathing procession and headed on down.

The odd thing was I didn't think we needed to be doing this. The building wasn't moving anymore. I heard no storm sounds and was sure whatever little thing had happened was over with.

When we finally reached the first floor, I was stunned to see smashed cars on the streets, and broken glass, pieces of roofing, and unidentifiable stuff littering the pavement. The glass-covered gazebo that domed the hotel bar was shattered; insulation fragments and dust covered everything. Threading our way through the broken glass, we were hustled into the ballroom with the warning that another tornado was due to touch down in a matter of moments. Several people were lying on the floor being fanned by friends, and one woman, who had suffered a heart attack, was later taken out by ambulance.

Well, Marilyn, so much for your assumption this wasn't a big deal, I thought sheepishly.

Three hours later the storms had passed and we were allowed to leave the ballroom. Fortunately, our hotel was pronounced structurally safe, the elevators were put back in operation, and we resumed our lives.

Later, as we watched the local television news and saw the horrific devastation resulting from the tornadoes, we realized how serious the storms had been. We also saw how fortunate we were in being spared greater destruction.

That night, lying in my bed listening for wind and wondering if the room was swaying again, I realized that a salvation message was tucked into the experience. When I had been staring out the window and then told to vacate the room, what if I had chosen not to? As it turned out, I would have survived.

But what if I had said, "Yes, I know there's a tornado out there. I can even see it. But I'm going to stay here anyway." It wasn't enough for me just to believe the tornado was raging through Nashville; I had to do something about what I believed.

Haven't you known people who have said, "Of course I believe in Jesus. I believe he is the Son of God"? But they didn't act on that belief; they just stood at the window seeing all the evidence but doing nothing about it. To become a child of God, I must believe Jesus is the Son of God. Then I must respond by receiving Jesus as Savior, accepting forgiveness of my confessed sin, and believing he has entered into my interior being, where he will stay with me through all the storms of my life.

As I was ruminating on these thoughts, Pat leaned over, turned on the light, and said, "Are you all right, Marilyn? You're whispering."

"Sure, I'm fine. I was just doing a bit of sermonizing, I guess."

"Really ... about what?"

"Acting on what you believe ... not being passive about it."

Studying the wall for a minute, she asked, "Do you think the building is swaying?"

"I don't believe so, but if I did, I'd act on it!"

Lord, thank you that you invite me to participate in becoming a member of your family. Help me never to lose sight of the importance of my believing and receiving. Enable me also to believe and receive the blessings you want to give me. I don't want to stand at the window and simply observe; I want to partake in a rich relationship with you. Amen.

Never Too Late

There is a time for everything, and a season
for every activity under heaven.
ECCLESIASTES 3:1

Come on, honey, you have to get out the door for
school." Hearing only silence, I popped into my eight-
year-old's room. Expecting to see Jeff hustling about in
an effort to leave, I was surprised to find him lying on his
bed, hands behind his head, staring at the ceiling.

"Sweetheart, are you okay? What are you doing just
lying on your bed?"

"I'm thinking."

"What are you thinking?"

"I'm thinking it's too late."

"Too late for what?"

"Going to school."

I sat down beside Jeff and wondered what was going
on in his mind. "Jeff, it really isn't too late. You have fifteen minutes. I'll drive you so you won't have to walk —
that way you'll have plenty of time."

"No, Mama, it's too late for my mind, and it's too late
for my body."

Biting my lower lip to prevent a giggle, I asked him
how long he thought his mind and body would be in that
state.

Sighing, he said, "Maybe all day."

Because he had never complained about this dire condition before, I let him stay home. We played a bit, went out to lunch, and ate ice cream in the park. I worried that I might be contributing to the let's-skip-school-and-play-instead syndrome. Jeff never complained again about his mind and body feeling too late, but went off to school the next day on schedule.

Many times in my life I too have wondered if it simply weren't too late for my mind and body. Some days I've thought not one idea in my head was worthy of anything but the compost pile. And some days I've thought I should just drape my body over the compost pile as well.

I am, however, always inspired by stories of people who refused to think it was too late for their minds and bodies. George Dawson from Dallas, Texas, certainly fits that description.* At the age of ninety-eight, George decided to learn how to read. He had kept his illiteracy a secret for nearly ten decades, but encouraged by a teacher from a local adult education program, George, after two years in literacy class, has learned to read at the third-grade level and write his name in cursive script. His pride and pleasure over acquiring these skills is so infectious that many people are enrolling in the school just to receive encouragement from George or to be with him.

Another never-too-late story is that of Grandma Moses, who, at the age of seventy-eight, had her first showing of paintings she had done from picture postcards and Currier and Ives prints. The following year she had fifteen one-woman art shows in both Europe and the United States. At ninety-two she wrote her autobiography, *My Life's History.* She received an honorary doctorate at age 100 and another at age 101.* I suppose she figured she had done enough, so she also died at age 101.

*"Happy," *People* (April 6, 1998), 112.

Closer to home is the story of Barbara Johnson, who wrote her first book when she was fifty. And now, at the age of seventy, she has more nonfiction books in print than just about anyone. She has given hope and encouragement to thousands of people through her Spatula Ministries and is a never-ending source of encouragement to my heart.

On a more personal note, my little Irish grandmother, at the age of 100, participated in a family reunion of her ten children, their spouses, and their children. The reunion was held on the old family farm where the ten "kids" had been raised. As they were organizing a baseball game to be played in the back field, my grandmother insisted on playing. When she hit a fly ball high into left field, her eldest son offered to run bases for her.

"Are you kidding, Basil?" she snorted, "You're eighty years old!"

Off she trotted. She lived to be 103.

God has created within all human beings a tremendous drive to survive and a capability to succeed to the level of our God-given gifts. Isn't it fantastic to realize that most of us have barely tapped into our potential? We could be creating and contributing so much more.

What keeps us from living out that potential? Do you suppose a few of us are lying on our beds with our hands behind our head and thinking, *It's too late for my mind, and it's too late for my body.*

Lord Jesus, don't let me miss what you have for me because I may have lost confidence in myself or in your enablement. May I be settled into the truth that I can indeed do all things through Christ who strengthens me. Then, Lord, softly push me out there; I promise I won't just lie on the bed. Amen.

Hey ... It's Not My Fault!

I acknowledge my transgressions.
PSALM 51:3 KJV

He's two-and-a-half years old, utterly adorable, and already has perfected the fine art of scapegoating. To my knowledge, no one has hunkered down with my grandson and explained the age-old practice of blaming others for his misdeeds. He seems to have taken to it quite naturally and, incidentally, does it well.

For the past few months, Ian has started to blame me for many of his minor sins.

"Ian," his mother, Beth, would say, "who told you it was okay to hide Halloween candy under your pillow?"

"Maungya."

"Ian, you don't eat dessert before you've finished your dinner."

"Maungya does!"

Last week Beth called to fill me in on a rather harrowing experience she had had when Ian overdosed on his multiple vitamin pill. As she was folding laundry in the bedroom, Ian managed to crawl up to the shelf where the vitamins were stored and break into the childproof bottle. Then he sauntered into the bedroom and sidled up to her, holding the half-empty container with his mouth crammed full of orange-flavored pills. Because excessive amounts of iron are toxic, and fearing that Ian might well have consumed enough iron to be dangerous, she called Poison Control and was advised to give him a dose of Ipecac, which would induce vomiting within twenty minutes. The experience was not pleasant, but he tossed up the pills in a timely manner and was soon playing with his backhoe and dump truck in the sandbox.

As Beth detailed all of this for me, Ian insisted he needed to talk to me immediately. Taking the phone from his mother, he stated in a reprimanding voice, "Maungya, you only take one vitamin pill! Did you hear me, Maungya?" In a short time he seemed to feel satisfied that he had sufficiently taken me to task, so he handed the phone back to his mother and went on about his important business.

I have giggled over Ian's stern discipline of me ever since. I have also spun off into a reverie about the whole blaming tendency that seems to be inherent in all of us. I've tried to figure out Adam's age when he blamed Eve for his disobedience to God's law. I figure he had been on the earth fewer days than Ian had when Adam pulled the stunt that ruined perfection for all of us. But, of course, it wasn't just Adam who did the blaming; Eve blamed the serpent for sweet-talking her into munching the forbidden fruit.

Blaming, refusing to take responsibility, passing the buck—whatever we call it—has an ancient history. Much as I hate to admit it, I too find myself eager to shirk responsibility for my various mistakes and shortcomings.

Just this week I was struggling with the temptation to wriggle out of responsibility for having missed a telephone radio interview about my new book. I wanted to do the interview; I simply forgot about it. When a couple of friends suggested we go to Houston's restaurant for their fabulous spinach-artichoke dip and chips, I was in the car before anyone else could put on her shoes.

The next day on a flight to a conference I found the interview confirmation sheet in my briefcase. Pondering the situation, I thought, *Do I call the station and confess that I was slathered to the elbows in spinach-artichoke dip at the exact time I was supposed to be talking to them?*

Though that's the truth, it doesn't make me look good. If I told them there must have been a mistake in dates, and I thought I was supposed to do the interview next week. . . . If I told them my secretary didn't inform me, and I knew nothing about the interview in the first place. . . . If I said a power outage occurred and all the phone lines were down for six hours. . .

The bottom line is, the truth doesn't make me look good, but not telling the truth makes me feel bad. What does one do? Well, one tells the truth, takes responsibility, looks bad but feels right morally. (Incidentally, I called the station and confessed. I waited for a cool reception to my irresponsible behavior. Instead, they warmly forgave me and set up another interview time. I like them.)

Why do you suppose we're so eager to blame instead of claim? My assumption is that we simply hate to look bad about anything to anyone — even ourselves. We don't want to be the bad guy — we want someone else to be.

Do you remember the term *scapegoat* in Leviticus 16? The custom was to have two goats. The first was sacrificed as a sin offering, and the second, the scapegoat, had the people's sins transferred to it by prayer and the laying on of hands. It's thought that the scapegoat was then taken into the wilderness never to be seen again.

How appealing. Put my "stuff" on the goat, send it away, and forget about it.

Of course, the symbolism is obvious as we realize that Christ became our sin bearer. He took on himself the sin of the world that we might become blameless. Great as that news is, I still have to take personal responsibility for my sin. I have to admit it to myself and then to God, and do so without the usual excuses.

Having done this, I can stop blaming and start claiming. Claiming what? Forgiveness! Feeling forgiven instead of full of excuses leads to freedom. Thank God we don't need a scapegoat; we have Jesus.

Lord Jesus, how graciously you provide for our every need. Thank you that because of the cross, I can truly be viewed as blameless in your sight. Enable me, Lord, to extend that kind of grace to myself. Enable me to extend that kind of grace to others. Amen.

Take Me Back

I the LORD do not change.
MALACHI 3:6

One of my favorite local stores is an English import shop that specializes in delicate bone china cups, teapots, little plates, and a myriad of other items crucial to the civilized preparation and drinking of tea. I was gingerly fingering a set of tiny Wedgwood butter dishes several weeks ago when the sound of twangy music began to penetrate my consciousness.

I paused, listened more closely, and thought, *Well, surely I'm not hearing "Church in the Wildwood." That doesn't fit this store.* "Shall We Gather at the River," "Nothing But the Blood of Jesus," and "O for a Thousand Tongues to Sing" followed.

I walked over to the very proper British owner and told her I loved the CD playing in the background. With her clipped, precise accent, she said, "Yes, isn't it quaint? We play it all the time."

The proprietor didn't seem to care about the message in those old hymns but instead seemed moved by the music's sounds and rhythms. The CD, entitled *Appalachian Memories,* featured handcrafted instruments: acoustic guitar, mandolin, Dobro, Autoharp, high-string guitar, and bass.

I was equally charmed by the sounds and rhythms; so forgetting all about the Wedgwood, I bought the CD and beat a hasty retreat home. It sounded even better on my sound system, and I found myself toe-tapping, grinning, and singing along from a wellspring of joy deep within me.

Just as the group and I were at the height of volume in "Love Lifted Me," Luci tapped at my window and wandered in. She watched me for a minute, looking perplexed and slightly uncomfortable.

Snapping off the CD player, I said, "I love that sound. Something about it pleases me way down to the core of my being!"

"It pleases you," she said uncertainly. Apparently, the music didn't have that effect on her. "Why?"

"As best I can figure, it takes me back to the little churches I grew up in."

Looking at the picture and title of the CD, she said, "You grew up in the Appalachians?"

"No . . . you know that."

"Well, what draws you?"

"I guess it's the Dobro!"

Laughing, Luci suggested that neither of us had ever heard of a Dobro, which, of course, was true. Nevertheless, every time I pop that CD into my machine, I grin and tap — and Luci disappears.

I think much of the soul-satisfying appeal comes from merely hearing those old hymns without orchestral adornment — just the straightforward, even plain sounds, somewhat like those Mrs. Farr used to coax out of the pump organ on Sunday mornings.

I experience a longing from time to time for a porch, a rocker, and a dog. I'd even like to look over at a barn with hay in it and cows languidly chewing their cud in the foreground. Maybe a few chickens could peck about, making those funny throat sounds that must mean something to their relatives. And, of course, parked over by the side of the house would be a dirty blue pickup truck with the windows rolled down. Aunt Bess, with her straw hat slightly askew, would sit in the truck all day just in case someone decided to drive to town.

I can picture all this so vividly because I've just described the farm that belonged to Leonard and Georgia Parker in Amboy, Washington, where I grew up. Their adult daughter, whom everyone called Aunt Bess, had an IQ equivalent to that of a six-year-old. She never seemed discouraged about anything. Every day she would sit in the pickup and walk back into the house each evening in time for supper. In the event someone went somewhere, she got to go along. Going or staying never seemed to alter her pleasure with each day.

The appeal of *Appalachian Memories* is that it takes me back to my childhood, a time when my life was less hurried and much less sophisticated. That rich and spiritually sweet world was peopled by folk who loved Jesus, loved one another, and let me drive their tractor.

Even though times and surroundings have changed, one thing never changes—Christ. He loved me then; he loves me now. He blessed me then, and he blesses me now. He is the solid rock upon which I stand now and forever. I love that constancy. What spiritual security we have. It's better than *Appalachian Memories*.

Hey, hear that sound? That's the Dobro and Autoharp playing "Victory in Jesus." Come on, let's tap, grin, and sing! We'll do it before Luci pops by.

Actually, I'll let you in on a little secret. She confessed she felt a bit dewy-eyed when she heard "At the Cross." Her daddy played a sweet Autoharp in his day. I think the sound took her back.

Lord, how comforting to know you are always there, living your life of love and victory through us no matter where we are or how old we are. You have promised never to leave us. Thank you for the security of your continual presence and your unchanging nature. Amen.

Life, Death, and Turtles

Jesus said, "Let the little children come to me."
MATTHEW 19:14

Y ou know, Elizabeth, I don't expect that child to live much beyond the age of six." My father, thinking I was safely out of earshot, made this dire prediction to my mother. He had just stopped the flow of blood from a deep cut to one of my knees and a cut on my right cheek, then he had successfully pulled out both front baby teeth, which had been dangling crookedly by thin membrane.

My four-year-old determination to fly like a bird had produced numerous other death-defying schemes, none of which was successful and all of which unsettled my parents. Each time they had rushed forward with bandages and Mercurochrome, wondering why they never saw me before I took my flying leaps.

As I lay on my bed obediently taking the rest for which I felt no need but recognized was purely for the benefit of my frazzled parents, I pondered my father's words. It took me awhile, but I ultimately figured out that if I lived to be six, that meant I had two more years to go. Actually, that seemed a lifetime to me. A lot of living was yet to be done, I reasoned, and if I died at six, well, so be it. I also decided that perhaps I'd focus my future energies on some goal other than flying.

I was five-and-a-half years old when Leroy Walker lumbered into my life. He was a turtle who had been tyrannizing Mrs. Boden's garden, and she said he could be mine if I simply promised to keep him away from her vegetables. That seemed an easy enough task, so I committed to keeping Leroy in my yard. But somehow life ceased to be a pleasure for Leroy in spite of the various green delicacies I provided him. Within a short time, he died.

My horror at his death was not that I had lost a beloved pet but that in a few weeks I would be six years old. That turtle and I were going out together, and I wasn't ready! I ran into the house, throwing myself into my mother's arms and telling her I didn't want to die, that the whole idea scared me, and I thought I was still too young for it.

After my mother assured me I wasn't going out at age six, she also assured me that death need not be something to fear. I would immediately be in God's presence whenever I died. Then we talked about how I could be assured I would go to heaven. When she explained to me that everyone in the world is born in sin and that sin is the part of you that wants to do the wrong thing, I felt not only a surge of understanding but also relief.

The idea of sin had never made sense to me until then. I knew full well something in me not only enjoyed doing the wrong thing but also sought it out.

A kid lived down the street from me who would do anything I suggested. One time I told him I was sure his mother would love it if he colored the wallpaper roses in the bathroom with her red lipstick. So he did and, of course, was in huge trouble as a result.

It bothered me that I would think up those kinds of things for him to do—that didn't seem to stop me, though. It had never occurred to me that my behavior was something everyone in the world experiences called "sin."

I figured my various flying schemes probably came from that sin root. I knew my parents didn't want me leaping off buildings, which was why I sneaked away to our neighbor's yard, which had an old garage I considered perfect as a launching pad. Neither my parents nor the neighbor had any idea I'd figured out how to open the gate that separated our properties. All of those schemes were tinged with that sense of wrongdoing, but now I had a name for the wrongdoing.

Even better, I learned there was a cure: his name was Jesus. When I asked him to come into my heart and clean up the sin mess, I was thrilled and relieved. I never doubted that he came, and I never doubted that I needed him. I will always carry that propensity to want to do the wrong thing . . . but now I will also always carry the cure within me.

Many times I've thought back to Leroy Walker and the pivotal role he played in my life. It's amazing to me that on his life and death rested my ultimate understanding about my own life and death. I was a little person to whom God sent a little messenger. He knew how to speak my language. I like that about him.

Perhaps God has designed a little messenger who will amble into your life with a pivotal message. How about that for an intriguing anticipation?

Thank you, Lord, for your gentle teaching and tender presence; thank you that your welcome and forgiveness extend to all persons at all times and in all stages of development. Amen.

Through It All

Even though I walk through the valley. . .
PSALM 23:4

One of my favorite words in the English language is *through*. I love it not for the way it sounds (like a muffled cough) or the way it looks (like two hills with a valley slung in between them), but for its meaning. It means "from beginning to end." That conveys encouragement to me.

It's not at all like the word *stuck*. *Stuck* sounds unattractive and feels discouraging. "It's a shame your tongue is stuck in that Coke bottle. . . . Hang on, and I'll get my slingshot." "You just missed the only flight out. I guess you're stuck here in Odorville for the next two days." "So sorry you didn't see the wet cement sign—you seem to be pretty well stuck."

Only last week the implications of *through* encouraged me as I valiantly tried to organize my records for Russ, my tax man. The job really shouldn't be that difficult, but I'm not a detail person, and I do pack around a number phobia. That adds up to a challenge.

For one thing, I'm in great need of a few write-offs. Since I'm a widow with no dependents, I suggested to Russ that perhaps it would be to my tax advantage to marry a man with a severely damaged liver who has fourteen physically challenged offspring who require daily physical therapy. That must have been a bad idea because Russ didn't pick up on it.

At any rate, I had been searching in vain for my new computer and printer receipts. (My old computer held such undisguised animosity toward me I simply had to terminate the relationship and start a new one.) I needed the receipts as proof for at least some teeny write-off but couldn't find them. Of course I had receipts for my new air conditioner as well as the Teledyne Water Pic showerheads for the bathrooms.

Comfort came as I nestled in with the word *through*. "Marilyn, you will get through all this muddle. You are not stuck here: This experience has an end. . . . You just aren't there yet!"

Last weekend I was flying back to Palm Desert from Chicago and made the mistake of asking my seat partner if she had had a good weekend. For more than three hours I heard about her sister-in-law's insensitivity, her husband's childlike dependence on his mother, the irresponsible way he handles money, his ex-wife's whining demands, and my seat partner's increasingly severe colitis. She leaned in closer and closer to me with each revelation, and I leaned farther and farther into the aisle. One painful encounter with the beverage cart threw me back into place quickly.

I don't normally mind these kinds of encounters—even though the woman barely came up for a breath the entire trip. But I was especially fatigued that day and found myself lacking the emotional stamina to keep a good attitude about her relentless negativity. What encouraged my spirits was the knowledge that ultimately I would get through the trip—I wasn't stuck with this woman forever.

For years my spirits have been buoyed by the concept of the word *through,* but I learned an even deeper understanding during my husband, Ken's, battle with cancer. I had promised him that he would not die in a hospital but that every effort would be made for him to remain at home. I determined to walk through every phase of that final journey with him.

On the morning he died, our daughter, Beth, and I were on either side of his bed, literally talking him into eternity. But what struck me as he took his final breath was that I could walk only so far through the experience with him. Earthbound limits were placed on me. I was, in essence, stuck here.

Psalm 23 says, "Even though I walk through the valley of the shadow of death, I will fear no evil, for you are with me." The only One able to walk through the valley with Ken was the Shepherd. The eternal truth, "You are with me," can be ascribed only to God.

I find that truth comforting. Yes, the word *through* means there will be an end to whatever is happening with me on this earth. But an even greater promise in that word is that when God walks me through, he suffers no human limitation; there is no separation from him. While God is with me in all my earthly "throughs," I'm heading for that final walk through, and we're doing it together!

The promise, Lord, of your continual and unfailing presence with me as I walk through the challenges of life restores and encourages my soul. Thank you for providing that which no one else can. Only you can see me through. Help me today to do just that. Amen.

Princess Fur-Face

I do not at all understand the mystery of grace—
only that he meets us where we are
but does not leave us where he found us.

ANNE LAMOTT

Whad'ya say we change the furniture around?" Ken queried one Saturday morning as we were finishing our last cups of coffee and tea. "Let's put the couch by the window and the two chairs facing the fireplace." I had learned years before to trust Ken's fine eye for furniture placement.

"Sounds good to me, Babe," I said, "but do you have the stamina for Ashley's neurotic response?"

Ashley was our cocker spaniel, who reacted strongly against all visual changes. She wanted things to remain in their accustomed spots. If they didn't, she had one of her "spells." It didn't matter how big or small the change; each warranted a protest. Let me give you an example.

A friend popped in on me one morning and for some reason just dropped her purse in the middle of the floor as we made our way to the "chat chairs." Several moments later Ashley, who hated to miss anything, came trotting into the room. Spotting my friend's purse in the middle of the floor, she skidded to a stiff-legged halt, stared briefly at the purse, and went into a dramatic fit of barking. Slowly circling the purse, she barked, growled, and scowled until my friend finally placed her purse behind the chair. Gradually Ashley settled down, but it was obvious the visit was ruined for her.

As Ken pondered the price to be paid for furniture rearrangement, he noted that Ashley was out on the deck dozing in the sun. She might not notice what was going on until the dastardly deed was done.

Several hours later Ashley roused herself from her siesta and ambled into the house. She immediately assessed that unauthorized changes had occurred in her absence. After barking herself nearly hoarse, she flounced out of the living room and stayed in her "sleep area" for several days. We delivered her food and water. Gradually she came to realize that the couch was now in a far better spot for her because she was able to see out the window. (Of course she was allowed on the furniture!) This made it possible for her to visually patrol the neighborhood without leaving the comforts of home.

Perhaps the greatest trauma Princess Fur-Face had to endure was when we got a new car. Ashley's sleep area was in a small room adjoining the garage, and although the car wasn't fully visible to her, it was close by.

On the first night of their cohabitation, Ashley, who had not yet been introduced to the new car, scampered down the stairs to bed as was her custom. We stood behind the closed door holding our breath. No sound . . . no barking . . . no response at all. Ken's theory was that because it was dark, Ashley couldn't see the car. Our intention was later, in the daylight, to gradually coax her into an accepting relationship with the new vehicle.

Around 1 A.M. we were awakened by the sound of frantic, ferocious barking. Ashley had discovered the car. Fearing she'd disturb the neighbors, Ken flew down the stairs, scooped up Ashley along with her bed, and deposited her in our room, something Ken normally refused to do. She grumbled and complained the rest of the night, but at least she didn't bark.

Because Ken drove the car to work during the day, I had no opportunity to ease Ashley into a spirit of charitableness about the car. Each night she seemed to forget about the alien in the garage when she first went to bed, then she rediscovered it sometime after midnight.

At 2:00 A.M. on the fourth night of Ashley's histrionics, Ken exasperatedly dragged himself out of bed and announced he had just come up with a plan requiring both of us to get dressed and take Ashley for a ride.

"Are you going to dump her out of the car somewhere in another county?" I asked cautiously as I threw on jeans and a sweatshirt.

"Trust me" was all he said.

Ken thrust a squirming, growling, barking cocker into my arms, and we got in the monster car to begin what Ken said would be the "taming ride." For at least an hour Ashley was a bundle of growling rigidity in my arms. With the radio playing soft music and both of us stroking Ashley with words of love and encouragement (none of which we felt at that moment), Ashley began to relax. An hour and a half later and miles from home, she went limp in my arms and fell asleep. From that moment on, Ashley had peace about her metal roommate. In fact, one of her favorite activities became riding in that car.

I hate to tell you how closely I identify with Ashley at times. There are God-gifts I have fought fervently, only to find that once I yield my resisting spirit I reap incredible benefits. For example, I certainly don't overtly resist the concept of grace, but I've tried to earn it a million times. I seem to cling tenaciously to the mistaken notion that I've got to be good enough in order to deserve grace. How many times does God have to hold my rigidly resisting spirit until finally, with celestial music in my ears, I relax and embrace his gift?

Ashley learned with just one ride.

No eye has seen, no ear has heard, no mind has conceived what God has prepared for those who love him.
1 CORINTHIANS 2:9

Box Seats Grace

A good sleep is grace and so are good dreams.
Most tears are grace. The smell of rain is grace and
somebody loving you is grace.

FREDERICK BUECHNER

In the California desert where I live, golf and tennis are popular sports and attract top professionals from all over the world for competitive play. I was chomping at the bit to get seats for this year's Evert Cup, but the tennis event had been sold out for months. My dear friend and faith connoisseur extraordinaire, Ney Bailey, knew how much I wanted to go. On Tuesday evening she announced that she was going to get tickets for Wednesday.

I swallowed a derisive snort and tried tactfully to point out that the huge SOLD OUT sign at the tournament entrance had a pretty clear message. Without the slightest hint of spiritual superiority, Ney said, "I've been talking to God about this, Marilyn, so I'm going to the ticket window early in the morning to see what happens."

"See what happens?" I responded with more than a smidgen of skepticism. "Do you expect God to be there just waiting for a missionary type and her little-of-faith friend to show?" Ney smiled that serene smile of hers and told me to keep my phone line clear the next morning between 8:00 and 8:30.

The phone rang at 8:13 and a jubilant Ney announced that not only did she get seats, she got center court box seats. I let out a "Yahoo!" that I'm sure unsettled my neighbors. Within minutes I'd packed my hat, sunscreen, dark glasses, and water and was out the door to meet my miracle-working friend.

As we waited for the first match of the day to begin, I asked Ney what God had looked like when he handed her the tickets. "Well, actually it was a woman in a green T-shirt who handed me the tickets," she said. We decided that image of God might not be well received in most Christian circles; perhaps it would be wise to keep this revelation to ourselves.

With great enthusiasm Ney then explained that some people had given up their box seats for that day with instructions for the folks at the ticket window to sell them. Because Ney was first in line, the seats were sold to her!

As the day progressed and we watched some of the finest tennis I'd seen in years, I kept saying to God, "Thank you, thank you, thank you! You know how I adore tennis. You know how I adore being outside in this gorgeous desert sunshine. You know I didn't want to be inside at my desk writing. I don't quite get it, but thank you, thank you, thank you!"

That evening as Ney and I were enjoying a late dinner, I once again shared with her what has been a spiritual conundrum to me most of my adult life: To what degree is God active in the minutiae of daily living? I wobble back and forth on this issue. Of course I can and do talk to him about everything—that's part of maintaining my spiritual connection. And of course I know he loves me and cares about all facets of my experience. But tennis tickets . . . do I really take *that* request to him? It almost seems like magical thinking to pray for tickets, and, when we get them, assume God brought it about. It makes more sense to me that whoever owned those seats woke up with a debilitating sinus infection, thus freeing the seats for us.

As Ney and I tossed this subject around, she said something, as she has so many times in our twenty-two-year friendship, that made me suddenly very quiet at the center of my soul: "I learned years ago not to edit my prayers." She explained that her job is to "make her requests known," as a child would, and then, no matter the result, trust that God is praised and honored. "Like a father, it pleases him to give good gifts to his children," Ney said. "And, Marilyn, God gifted both of us with a great day of tennis! Our job is simply to unwrap his gracious gift . . . and enjoy!"

There was no way I could argue with that. But, you know, I can't help but feel bad for that person with the severe sinus infection.

And if you hardhearted, sinful men know how to give good gifts to your children, won't your Father in heaven even more certainly give good gifts to those who ask him for them?

MATTHEW 7:11 TLB

Quackers

> The cross means that intimacy with God
> is wildly, wonderfully possible.
> TIMOTHY JONES

I love out-of-the-norm experiences that feed the quirky side of my soul. So when I found out that an upcoming Women of Faith conference was to be held in Memphis, Tennessee, and we'd be staying at the Peabody Hotel, I was delighted.

You see, the Peabody is home to a little flock of ducks that put on a show each day for an audience of hotel guests who apparently have nothing better to do than to set their watches by Duck Time. Just before eleven o'clock each morning, a red carpet is laid out from the elevator to the marble fountain in the middle of the hotel lobby. At exactly eleven, the elevator doors burst open, and five ducks dash through them, race down the carpet at top speed, and then pitch headfirst into the fountain water. They swim around in there all day until the red carpet is once again stretched out at five o'clock. They waddle back down the carpet into the elevator where they're whisked up to their little duck penthouse for the night. Once there, I envision them snacking on duck pâté (ducks have no loyalty—the pâté is probably the bird that moved too slowly) and quacking about the day's performance.

Seeing the feathered little ruffians' escapades for myself gave me an enormous giggle. In talking briefly with one of the hotel personnel, I commented on the speed and energy with which the ducks exited the elevator in their pell-mell race for the fountain. He told me I'd probably burst through the doors too if I had a trainer with a little stick behind my back. Being assured that the ducks were well-treated and the stick was only a symbol of rarely used encouragement, I threaded my way through the people-jammed lobby to the gift shop, where I belonged.

Oddly enough, though, the image of the ducks with a stick poised at their backs to ensure good performance stuck with me. How grateful I am that God doesn't use such means to keep me in line! Instead, he extends a luxurious grace that allows me to stay on the elevator if I want to — or sprawl out on the red carpet until day's end. God's grace is not about a performance and a stick.

In fact, grace is about a loving father who not only does not demand performance but seeks to support us in what we do. Second Chronicles 16:9 assures us: "For the eyes of the LORD move to and fro throughout the earth that He may strongly support those whose heart is completely His" (NASB).

What a fantastic image! God searching, watching, seeking us out wherever we are on the earth. And for what purpose? That he might give us support! Support ... not condemnation. Support ... not criticism. Support ... not rejection. God searches for us, not wielding a stick but offering encouragement.

There are those believers for whom that message of grace does not compute. It defies logic; it can't really be true; and certainly it can't be meant for the likes of us. Those are the people we see day in and day out, living their lives with a sense of frantic urgency, afraid that at any moment they're going to feel the stick. But God says to them: "Come to Me all you who are weary and heavy laden, and I will give you rest" (Matt. 11:28 NASB).

Where there is grace, there is no stick. Instead there is rest . . . and sweet support.

Before this faith came, we were held prisoners by the law, locked up until faith should be revealed. So the law was put in charge to lead us to Christ that we might be justified by faith. Now that faith has come, we are no longer under the supervision of the law.

GALATIANS 3:23–25

Cataplexy

There is nothing but God's grace.
We walk upon it; we breathe it; we live and die by it.
ROBERT LOUIS STEVENSON

The subject of computers seems to elicit a deeply felt but broad range of emotions. There are those who love their computers with such devotion they don't leave home without them. There are others who love their computers on some days and hate them on other days. Their feelings range from deep affinity to potent animosity.

I find this breadth of emotion fascinating as well as mystifying. To me it is so simple to have only one emotion regarding computers — that of loathing. I have fussed about my troubled relationship with the personal computer before; however, I recently discovered a word that accurately describes the physical and emotional condition created in me by computer proximity or my attempt to use a computer.

The word is *cataplexy*. It means "a sudden state of immobility caused by extreme emotional stimulus." I love that word! It makes me feel so understood. There is such security in knowing that a label exists for my affliction. And yet there is no pleasure in the condition. Therefore, I've had to determine a way to avoid cataplexy at all costs.

Obviously, since my computer is the only stimulus in my life that provokes cataplexy, I need to keep my computer out of sight and out of reach. That avoidance guarantees my good health. A simple solution, but here's the problem: pride. I'm not only embarrassed by my cataplexy, I'm embarrassed that an electronic box can reduce me to such a state.

Most of the other women I know have generally loving, warm, reciprocal relationships with their computers. When we come from all corners of the U.S.A. for planning meetings, each whips out an extension cord, claims her very own wall socket, and plugs in. In the midst of all this preparatory frenzy, I'm rifling through my purse in an effort to find a pen just in case I too might take notes during the meeting. This is hard on my pride, but I've managed to bear up under it. My techie friends are kind.

But just last week I experienced a breakthrough that will not only eliminate all future threat of cataplexy but of humiliation as well. (By the way, humiliation has its root in pride.)

My dear friend Patsy, who for six months of the year lives only one street away from me, wandered into my house on Wednesday. She stopped dead in her tracks (much like our dog Ashley used to do when we rearranged the furniture). Staring at the object on my counter, she said, "What's that?"

"It's a typewriter. You may remember seeing one at the Smithsonian when we were in Washington, D.C., last winter."

"Ummm, do you use it for something, Marilyn?"

Reluctantly I confessed that when writing a book, I first scratch my thoughts out on a yellow legal pad. Then I type my scratches on my typewriter. I give my typed pages to my friend Pat, who retypes my words into her computer, and they end up on a square doodad. But she also sends them somehow to the computer of my editor, where they wait to be discovered.

Patsy's look of compassion as she listened to the pitiful rendering of my writing process nearly reduced me to tears. "Honey," she said, "you wait right here. I'll be back in three minutes. I want to read you something."

She returned with a magazine about how to write and publish fiction. From it she read to me the experience of a best-selling fiction writer who cannot bear computers and is terrified that typewriters will one day cease to be manufactured. This author literally stockpiles typewriters from Staples. (I had just purchased my third typewriter the day before Patsy dropped by.) The writer went on to say that she doesn't want to lose any of her crossed-out words from her legal pad in case she should decide later to use them after all.

Yahoo! My feelings exactly! I've rummaged through discarded scratchings a thousand times, convinced that whatever it was I wrote an hour ago is better than what I wrote two seconds ago. A computer would disdainfully destroy my scratchings forever. The yellow pad gently and without judgment preserves them for me in the event that I might someday want them. So nurturing.

When I finished that little therapy session with Patsy, my shame was banished and my dignity was restored! She extended to me a most wonderful and refreshing cup of grace. She didn't even hint that I was pitiful, technologically challenged, or hopelessly behind the times. Instead, Patsy encouraged me by comparing my archaic writing methods with those of one who just happens to be a best-selling author and with whom I might one day fight over the world's last remaining typewriter!

Patsy, your style reminds me of God's.

God is our Light and our Protector. He gives us grace and glory.　　　　　　　　PSALM 84:11 TLB

Smoke Travels

God's grace makes us worthwhile and valuable for who we
are, and not because of what we successfully accomplish.
DAVID SEAMANDS

One of my childhood heroes was a woman I met only
once. She wore outlandishly bright colors and spiked
high-heeled shoes, sported mounds of dyed red hair, and,
most memorable, belched frequently. She was married
to the conference superintendent, one of the local admin-
istrators of the church denomination in which my father
pastored.

I met Mrs. Justin when she and Dr. Justin came to our
home for dinner. My mother had coached me ahead of
time, warning that Mrs. Justin had some kind of digestive difficulty that caused her to belch whenever the need
should arise. When that happened, I was not to wheel
around and stare or giggle. That was a tall order, but I
promised.

Dr. Justin had already presented a challenge to my
self-control on two occasions when he had guest-pastored
at Dad's church. He wore the worst-looking toupee one
could imagine. Not only was gleaming scalp visible under
its ill-fitting edges, but it was never centered—a fact that
mystified me. To my child logic, it seemed perfectly simple for him to center the hairpiece by using his nose as a
marker. Apparently that obvious solution had never been

considered because the toupee consistently veered either to the left or the right, especially when he energetically expressed his sermon's main points.

When the Justins arrived for dinner, I was laboring under so many restrictions on my behavior that I felt tense. Mrs. Justin lived up to her belching reputation throughout the meal, but I was relieved to find that I didn't have any desire to giggle. There was something rather poignant about her. She never entered into any of the conversation but seemed instead to be in her own noisy little world. I ultimately decided she didn't have a digestive difficulty at all: she was simply bored. I certainly was. But, of course, I didn't dare use her remedy.

At the conclusion of the meal I was excused to go upstairs to my room. My intention was to stretch out on my bed for a good read. As I switched on the radio, I saw the Lucky Strike cigarette I had scooped up from our neighbor's driveway the day before. Since the cigarette was so clean and tidy, I'd tucked it behind my radio ... perhaps for a time such as this. After all, I was still feeling a trifle tense, and people claimed to feel more relaxed after a cigarette. Maybe I needed that more than my book.

I'd never smoked, and it didn't occur to me that any particular skill was necessary. As I lit the cigarette and drew the smoke into my mouth, I didn't know what to do next. Involuntarily I gagged and coughed as smoke came out of every orifice above my neckline. *How do people get the smoke to exit only through their nostrils in that steady trail that looks so effortless?* I wondered. Try as I might, I could only spew ghastly billows of smoke from my mouth. I was not finding this a pleasant activity, and it certainly wasn't relaxing me. In fact, I was feeling increasingly nauseated and light-headed.

It never crossed my mind that the smoke would slip under my closed door, glide down the stairs, and quietly enter the living room where Dr. Justin sat talking church business with my parents. It wasn't until my mother's disapproving face appeared at my door that I realized I might soon be facing an indictment.

Shortly after, I was invited downstairs to say good-bye to the Justins. As I awkwardly shook hands with each of them, Mrs. Justin leaned down and whispered in my ear, "Don't worry about your smoking, honey. I started at an early age myself."

I realize now that Mrs. Justin was probably as off-center as her husband's toupee, but nonetheless she extended unexpected grace to me. In that era, smoking was considered completely taboo by most Christians. What Mrs. Justin's comment did for me was to make me feel still connected to others instead of ostracized as a smoking little sinner.

My brief exchange with the belching but gracious Mrs. Justin provided an early lesson about God's grace and God's family. I believe that one of the best ways we extend the gift of grace is by remaining connected to others when they blow it. God himself continues to love us with the same gracious intensity even when we fail. No matter how huge or small our transgression, he will absolutely stay with us, love us, encourage us, and lead us back to healthy behavior. That's what he wants us to do for each other.

Incidentally, I haven't smoked since.

A bruised reed he will not break, and a smoldering wick he will not snuff out.

ISAIAH 42:3

Contagious Grace

Grace is too unpredictable, too lavish, too delicious
for us to stay sober about it.
LEWIS B. SMEDES

On a recent Sunday morning, I was reminded of how contagious grace is when one believer lives it out in front of others. Sweet nostalgia swept over me as I joined the church congregation in singing "How Great Thou Art" under the direction of Cliff Barrows. My mind was flooded with memories of that dear man when, at least forty years before, I sang in the volunteer choir for the Billy Graham Crusade in Portland, Oregon, and then ten years later in the choir in Anaheim, California.

Now, with the same sweet spirit of one whose ministry and life so winningly radiates the grace of God, Cliff Barrows led us in some of the great hymns of faith. As we completed the last verse of "I Love to Tell the Story," Dr. Barrows stepped behind the pulpit, opened his Bible, and began his sermon. I was so aware that this man was an icon of the Christian faith, and I felt privileged to hear him. Coupled with these very genuine feelings of appreciation, my memory served up an experience with Dr. Barrows that I had not thought of in years.

I was chairperson of Fullerton's Christian Women's Club and thrilled that Dr. Barrows was to be our December guest speaker. The night before that Christmas luncheon,

I was increasingly agitated as I tried to think of a worthy introduction for this dearly loved man. Everything I thought to say sounded so flat, so dull, so uninspiring. My husband, Ken, tried to encourage me out of my dithering state with phrases like "It'll come to you" or "It's only an introduction, Marilyn."

When nothing came, I finally went to bed and drifted into a most graphic and specific dream about the luncheon. In that dream, shortly after Dr. Barrows started speaking, he slipped a little silver flask out of his breast pocket. He took a quick sip and then replaced the flask. Several times throughout his speech he repeated this little maneuver, and as his words became increasingly incoherent, everyone in the room began glowering at me as if I were the one responsible for the flask and its effects. One by one the women began gathering up their belongings and, with withering expressions shot in my direction, exited the room. Within a few moments Dr. Barrows and I were the only two left. When he took full notice of that fact, he patted my shoulder and said, "It's just as well, Marilyn, my flask is empty anyway."

I awakened the next morning giggling over the implausibility of Cliff Barrows's behavior depicted in my dream. I asked Ken if he thought I could use it in my introduction. With one of those "Are you out of your mind?" looks, Ken swept on out of the house and headed for work.

Several hours later as I stood to introduce Dr. Barrows, I decided to risk telling the dream. The women enjoyed its obvious absurdity but were slightly restrained in their responses since they weren't sure how it was being received by Dr. Barrows. When he stood up, he first smiled warmly at everyone and then reached into his vest pocket, pulled out an imaginary flask, threw his head back, made a slurping sound, and sighed with satisfaction as his audience burst into peals of appreciative laughter. Everyone loved him! We loved not only his winsomely delivered, God-centered message but also his freedom to be playful and not hung up with images or appearances.

In direct contrast to his contagious freedom was the note slipped to me from a woman at the luncheon. She wrote that she felt joking about the flask was inappropriate for a Christian environment and that she was deeply offended. This was not the first note I had received from her, and certainly not the first criticism. It's quite possible that her grim-faced approach to life was rooted in some deep pain to which I'm not privy, but I find it sad that her life seems to revolve around the externals of what she perceives to be "the faith." Monitoring and reporting infractions of the "rules" keeps her more engaged than does the sweetness of God's grace.

I worry sometimes that we as believers are more concerned with the appearance of righteousness than with the inner acquisition of righteousness. Celebrating the gift of grace means freeing oneself from the shackles of performance and luxuriating in the circumference of God's lavish acceptance. Now that's a gift worth toasting!

I am come that they might have life, and that they might have it more abundantly.

JOHN 10:10 KJV

The Boy Next Door

She had *what?*"
"Ruptured silicone implants."

"What did she do?"

"Had 'em taken out."

"So other than her being flat-chested, what's the problem?"

"A bunch of physical symptoms. At first a doctor summed it up by telling her she had an immune disorder but didn't know its cause."

"What does that have to do with silicone implants?"

"She later learned that apparently silicone is toxic."

"I read that it isn't."

"She read the same thing."

"So what's the deal with her?"

"She's getting better; the improvements are slow, but they're happening."

That mini-dialogue about me has occurred to varying degrees between various people who have known something was "off" with me, but didn't know what. For a while I didn't know what either. One sure way to put someone into a coma is to launch into a detailed health report, so I'll spare you that. I do, however, want to discuss my personal experience because almost everything else I write in this book springs from what God is teaching me in it. But before we get too spiritual, I'll pull aside the privacy curtain and tell you how all this came about in the first place.

Twenty-eight years ago my neighbor, Mary, dashed across the street to tell me she was getting a fantastic deal on silicone implants from the plastic surgeon for whom she worked.

"But," I said, "isn't his specialty noses? He fixes noses, not bosoms."

"I guess he wanted to branch out or something. Anyway, he took the training, he's certified, board-approved, and I'm losing my boy-next-door look in the morning!"

Having sported the boy-next-door look myself as long as I could remember, I was envious.

"So, how come you're getting a deal, Mary. What does that mean?"

"Well, my doctor needs the experience, so I get the surgery at his cost. He told me he would offer the same deal to a few of my friends if they were interested."

That evening I brought up the subject to Ken, who was mildly horrified by the "I'll give you a deal while I learn the procedure" mentality. I pointed out to Ken that there was some similarity in the shapes of noses and bosoms and maybe it wasn't really such a stretch to move from the nose to the. . . . Ken was not convinced.

Because I couldn't rid myself of the appeal of sporting feminine curves instead of boyish lines, Ken did some investigating about Mary's doctor and learned he had impeccable credentials, as well as an excellent reputation with other doctors. With Ken's reluctant approval I had the breast surgery done by the nose man.

The results were exceedingly gratifying. Even Ken became an enthusiast. (I must admit, however, that the flaring little nostrils at the base of each breast were a bit distracting.) The reality is, I had no problems with them at all. In contrast, a friend of mine paid a breast augmentation specialist four times what I did and had to have the surgery redone twice. The first time, one breast pointed slightly north and the other south. The second time, they both pointed a little south. I told her she should have hired a nose man.

Seven months ago, I yielded to the persistent nagging of my OB-GYN and got a mammogram. (I had not had one in twenty years. I was afraid that Gestapo technique might cause my noses to run.) With ill-disguised horror, the doctor showed me on a sonogram that both implants were ruptured and that my chest cavity was full of free-floating silicone. She told me to "run, not walk" to a surgeon for removal of the mess.

Assuming that my task was merely to get the operation and return to boyishness, I was stunned to learn that my entire body was splattered with stray silicone—the greatest concentration being in the lymph nodes under both arms. While there are many women with silicone implants who have no symptoms of toxicity, my recovery from all that floating poison, in spite of the removal of the implants, has proven to be slow and, at times, debilitating.

My intent in writing this is not to become a poster child for silicone survivors. Silicone, whether it is indeed toxic or not, is a subject of medical controversy and increasingly serious inquiry as well as research. My intent is to provide background for some of the other things I've written in this book and, more important, to underscore the reality of God's boundless love in the midst of our messes in life.

It would make perfect sense to me if God's response to my current needs was expressed with statements like: "Well, Marilyn, after all, you brought this whole health crisis on yourself. You're simply experiencing the consequences of your own vanity, your poor decisions nearly thirty years ago. Here you are struggling with challenges that have their origin in your worldly, self-absorbed preoccupation with something as superficial as not wanting to look like the boy next door. Tsk, tsk, tsk."

Those messages, which I give myself, have never once been echoed by God. In stark contrast I consistently receive the encouragement and solace of his nonjudgmental love and support:

> I cried out, "I'm slipping!" and your unfailing love,
> O LORD, supported me.
>
> PSALM 94:18 NLT

Nothing I have done as a faltering human being merits what I receive daily from him. He even says:

> The steps of the godly are directed by the LORD.
> He delights in every detail of their lives.
> Though they stumble, they will not fall,
> for the Lord holds them by the hand.
>
> PSALM 37:23 NLT

What is so astounding to me is that God does not say, "As long as you don't stumble, Marilyn, I'll hang around and be supportive." Rather, he says he *delights* in every detail of my life — not because the details are always delightful but because he is my hand-holding God who walks with me through the events of my life no matter how foolish or misguided my steps may be. In fact, he uses those very experiences to deepen and strengthen my relationship with him. Scripture reminds me of why he cares so deeply about what is going on in my world.

> The LORD still waits for you to come to him so he can show you his love and compassion. For the LORD is a faithful God. Blessed are those who wait for him to help them.
>
> ISAIAH 30:18 NLT

How blessed each of us is to have such a compassionate, faithful God! When we feel like we've made a mess of things (even if it's only by mistake), we can be sure that our ever-waiting Lord will not only remove the mess, but he will also show us the fullness of his boundless love as we wait for rescue.

As for me, I thank God that many of my troublesome symptoms are beginning to lessen; my stamina and overall health are returning. No matter what the future holds, no matter what shape my body parts are in, I know God's love for me will never waver.

Flat or "busty," you are loved!

"I Like That about Him"

Last summer I was with my two grandsons and their mama at a city park. I was swinging two-year-old Alec in my lap, knowing full well I should not be swinging anyone, anywhere, anytime. Swings, cars, planes — almost all motion makes me nauseated. (I am such a travel pleasure.)

The continual back-and-forth motion was getting to me, but I hated to stop simply because of the obvious delight Alec was experiencing: Gamma's lap, a soft breeze in his face, and the security of knowing he could not fall as long as I held him. Little did he know that I was on the verge of losing my grip on him as well as my grip on lunch.

Yielding to the practical concerns about to overwhelm me, I stopped the swing, set Alec on his feet, and attempted to get on my own. As I sank to the grass under a tree, Alec flexed his little knees, peered up into my face, and asked, "You in bad shape, Gamma?"

"I'm not really in bad shape, honey. Gamma just doesn't swing well."

After several moments of reflection Alec asked, "Does you forget how?"

Slightly insulted at his insinuation that age and memory loss had taken their toll, I told him I remembered how to swing, but that I really don't like to swing. (It didn't seem prudent to get into the whole nausea topic.) My displeasure with swinging appeared momentarily to mystify Alec, but apparently he came up with an interpretation that was satisfactory. He went over to the slide and announced to big brother Ian that "Gamma 'barrassed."

"Why?" Ian asked.

"Can't swing," Alec replied without compassion.

Ever the sensitive little man, Ian came over and sat beside me on the grass. Taking a different tack than his brother, Ian asked if I was afraid of swinging and was that why I was sitting on the grass. I remembered he was at least eighteen months old before he would even venture near a swing; for some reason he was terrified of them. Assuming I was suffering from his early fears, Ian then asked if I thought Jesus could help me.

That question put me into an immediate theological bind because if I said, yes, Jesus could help me, I would probably need to get back on the swing as evidence of my faith. If I said no, I would be demonstrating limiting God in the small things (like swings) but implying that somehow he helped for the big things like . . . who knows where to draw the line? Is there a line? Mercy!

I came up with what I thought was a brilliant response, which kept me from theological jeopardy. I told Ian, "Jesus is helping me right now . . . this very minute as we sit on the grass."

Ian's little face relaxed and he said, "That's good . . . I like that about him."

Several months ago Ian, Alec, and their parents (my daughter, Beth, and her husband, Steve) moved to Palm Desert, California, where I live. They are only five minutes from me (eight if I miss the light at the intersection).

Last weekend Ian and I were sitting on my back patio looking out at the golf course and chatting about everything from why his mom should let him swim with or without her in the pool, to why he liked Tootsie Rolls better than suckers. He also wanted me not to worry about his teeth "'cause he was gettin' new ones anyway."

In the midst of this exchange there was sudden frantic chirping and flapping of wings from a nearby bird's nest that I'd observed a week ago. I was especially aware of this nest because I had watched the gardeners pruning the shrub in which the nest was located. They had carefully trimmed the bush, leaving a nonsymmetrical tuft of branches lurching off to the side that ensured the stability of the little hatching house nestled within. What could have appeared as evidence of bad eyesight on behalf of the gardeners was, in reality, sensitivity from their hearts. I had kept an eye on the energetic comings and goings of the little plant tenants ever since the pruning.

What had set the birds off was a poorly hit golf ball that ricocheted off the bush and then skipped into the duck pond a few feet away. Except for a few more bird complaints everyone settled down, including the golfer.

Ian was fascinated by the history of the little bird home and felt bad about their scare from the golf ball. Rising to the possibility of being a grandmother of spiritual influence, I decided to do a little sermonizing. I asked if he remembered talking to me about my supposed fear of swinging and that he'd questioned if I thought maybe Jesus could help me with that fear. He seemed to have no memory of the event, so I skipped to the present and said that Jesus cares if any of us is scared—not only grandmas but birds as well. Ian was more interested in returning to the subject of Tootsie Rolls, the swimming pool, and then a new topic: his friend's baby sister. Apparently both Ian and his friend thought the baby was boring. *So much for being a grandmother of spiritual influence,* I thought, as I empathized with Ian that the baby didn't even like trucks.

Several days later I popped in on the kids briefly to say hi and deliver a pocket full of Tootsie Rolls. As I was walking back to my car, Ian ran over to me, grabbed my hand, and said, "Maungya, you 'member that about Jesus and the birds at your house?"

"Yes," I said eagerly.

"Well, you know . . . I like that about him."

Moments later, as I sat in my favorite patio chair enjoying the delicious early evening grass smells and, of course, keeping an eye on the bird shrub, I was immersed in the tenderness of God's love. Psalm 50:11 states: "I know every bird of the mountains, and everything that moves in the field is Mine" (NASB).

Watching the busy shrub activity, I thought, *They don't even know . . . they haven't a clue that it is God who made them. It is God himself who delights in them and provides for them. They never need to be afraid.*

On the heels of those thoughts came the even sweeter reminder that Jesus expressed in Matthew 6:26: "Look at the birds of the air, that they do not sow, nor reap nor gather into barns, and yet your heavenly Father feeds them. Are you not worth much more than they?"

Ah, yes, I thought, sinking more deeply into my chair . . . *I like that about him.*

Our Father's love is
deeper and wilder than we typically imagine.

DUDLEY J. DELFFS

I like that about him!

Resign or Rejoice

Last week my grandson Ian, who will be five years old next month, asked his mother how to keep the Devil out of their house. My daughter, Beth, calmly responded that the best way to keep the Devil out of one's house is to have Jesus in one's heart. She explained how that could happen. Ian eagerly prayed a prayer inviting Jesus in and letting the Devil out.

Though I was thrilled to hear of Ian's prayer, I was troubled by the fears that prompted his decision. What had he heard or imagined or even experienced that gave rise to his fears? Ian's family environment is free of many of the "survival" needs common to some children's households, but nonetheless he was not feeling entirely safe.

Ian asked me yesterday if I ever watched Mr. Rogers. I told him I used to watch him with Beth. That information seemed to be more than he could sort out. Finally, he said softly, "Mr. Rogers is nice."

The longevity of the highly respected Mr. Rogers television show gives testimony to the need of children to experience an environment of calm assurance and soothing love. For decades Mr. Rogers has somehow managed to make the confusing complexities of life less threatening to children through singing songs and telling stories. With those songs and stories, children settle into an interior place where the prospect of love and security does not seem so improbable.

Recently I read some anonymous person's declaration to "resign" from adulthood and return to the magical, playful, "simple" world of an eight-year-old. "I want to make angels in the snow," he wrote. (Me too!) "I want to lie under a big oak tree and run a lemonade stand with my friends on a hot summer's day. I want to return to a time when life was simple . . . and all you knew was to be happy because you were blissfully unaware of all the things that should make you worried or upset."

As I reflected on Ian's feelings about the devil and Mr. Rogers, I meandered down memory lane, where so many of my own childhood insecurities first showed up. Like my dismal failure with a lemonade stand. Bobby Amdigger and I entered into this business venture with only two lemons between us. He said it didn't matter how many lemons we had as long as we threw lots of sugar and water into the jug. Apparently that was not a recipe favored by the local citizens.

Speaking of dismal failures, the memory of my third-grade math teacher standing beside my desk tapping it rhythmically with her ruler, saying repeatedly, "Think . . . think . . . think . . . " still makes me desperate for recess.

Then there was my fifth-grade tension over Marty Manson and if he liked me better than Dorothea Hootenpile. She was an adorable little girl whom all the boys liked. I was sure I saw a glow in Marty's eye when he looked at her, but he told me I would always be his best girlfriend because I could run faster than anyone in the school. Somehow that didn't give me sufficient confidence; I would rather have been cute and slow than skinny and fast.

When I first read that "resignation" piece I was charmed by the nostalgia of lying under big trees, making angels in the snow, and even the memory of my trying to bring order and sense and "success" to my little world as a child. But now I wonder if there was really such a time or place when innocence and simplicity existed to the exclusion of harsher realities? In other words, is life really "simple" at any age? I think sometimes we so long for what we've never known in this imperfect world that we gloss our history until we're convinced we did know it at one time, and if only we could return to it, all would be well. "The good ol' days" are often just a fabrication based on wishful thinking.

Dwight D. Eisenhower, our thirty-fourth president, said in reference to his childhood, "Our pleasures were simple — they included survival." In a similar vein, George F. Will stated, "Childhood is frequently a solemn business for those inside it."

Yes, Mr. Rogers is nice, the Devil's bad, ice cream's good, and broccoli's too green. Childhood events can be wonderful, but sometimes brutal. Adulthood is not that different. The bottom-line truth we all know is that we can't really resign from any phase of life.

But I don't think that's bad news. Because our future is utterly secure through Christ's sacrifice for our sins, we need not spend our adult lives longing for what we may or may not have had in terms of "perfection" and simplicity. We will experience all of that in eternity, where there is no nostalgic past or wishful future. When we reach our ultimate destination, with Christ in heaven, all time will be present tense; we'll live in a never-ending state of bliss that cannot be improved upon.

But what about the here and now? Are there no pleasures here, no rich and memorable moments? Of course there are! God loves us so lavishly and outlandishly that our blessings in life are too numerous to count — if we have eyes to see. But no human being, whether she is eight or eighty, has only good days. Returning to a "blissfully unaware" childlike state is not only impossible, but I think the longing itself is only a remnant of the righteous hunger for perfection that God planted in our eternity-bound souls. The good news is that the most incredible best that is yet to come is beyond even our incredible imagination!

In the meantime, I avoid old lemonade recipes, ruler-tapping authority figures, and men who won't admit they prefer women who are cute and slow. I move instead toward people with positive attitudes who realize that no matter where the Devil is at the moment, Jesus is everywhere all the time. Because the God in us is so much greater than any evil, sadness, failure, or fear in this world (1 John 4:4), you and I and little Ian can step up to whatever life holds with faith and boldness. God's love is big and strong enough to contain big people and small people at every stage of life. We don't have to resign.

> For God hath not given us the spirit of fear; but of power, and of love, and of a sound mind.
>
> 2 TIMOTHY 1:7 KJV

That truth encourages me to rejoice instead of resign!

Tip of the Pencil

How about that for a headline? This bizarre but true story details what happened when a Helena, Montana, boy bounced a football off the wall of his room, dove onto his bed to grab the ball, and somehow drove a pencil through his chest and into his heart.

His mother, responding to his frantic cries for help, dashed to his room and saw the pencil in her son's chest. As a nurse, she knew the worst thing she could do was to yield to the instinct to pull the pencil out of her son's body. To do so would release a torrent of blood, and he could quickly bleed to death. So, with stubborn intensity, she cupped one hand over the pink rubber eraser to prevent her panicked son from yanking it out, and with the other hand she dialed 911.

A CAT scan revealed that the pencil had not only pierced the child's heart, it had penetrated a valve. He would need open-heart surgery, which meant an airlift to the nearest cardiac surgeon and heart-lung machine one hundred miles away.

Three hours later the boy finally made it to the operating table. The doctor put the heart's right side into cardiac arrest, diverted the blood supply to the heart-lung machine, and began repairing the damage. After a successful surgery, the doctor reported that if the pencil had taken a slightly different path into the boy's body, it could have destroyed far more of the heart's blood-pumping machinery. Also, because of the mother's levelheaded reaction in not pulling out the pencil, the blood loss was so minimal that the patient needed no transfusion during surgery. Amazingly there was no infection, no contamination from pencil lead, and no permanent heart damage. In less than three weeks the boy was itching to get back to school.

I've found myself pondering this dramatic story from a number of different angles. For one thing, I'm so impressed by the mother's ability to see beyond the horrific circumstances and do what was best for her child. In her ability to recognize what would be for her son's ultimate good, she fought off the instinct to remove the arrow-like pencil. That firm decision saved his life. At the time it must have made no sense to the child, and in his near hysteria he could well have wondered why his mother seemingly didn't help him. Why did he have to endure such pain and fear? Why the wait? It made no sense. Unlike his mother, the boy didn't see the big picture.

How natural of us all to want an immediate removal of the arrows that pierce our hearts, the pain that consumes our bodies, or the despair that wraps around our souls. We cry out as the psalmist did: "O God, do not remain quiet; do not be silent and, O God, do not be still" (Ps. 83:1 NASB). In other words, *Do something, and please do it NOW.*

The problem with my desire for a quick fix is that I can miss the big picture of what only God knows is for my better good. That good is frequently accomplished by putting me in waiting mode — and I don't like to wait. I pound on heaven's door sometimes, begging for God to *get on with it,* but God's love is stubborn. It is also merciful. When I must wait, I've experienced the truth of yet another of the psalmist's prayers: "When my anxious thoughts multiply within me, thy consolations delight my soul" (Ps. 94:19 NASB).

It is often when I am in deepest need, when my anxiety-riddled thoughts threaten to overwhelm me, that God soothes and consoles me. Those times are the sweetest I have ever known, and yet, even knowing that, I still want the quick fix. However, God knows better what will develop my trust, increase my faith, and enlarge my spiritual understanding. In his perfect love for me, in his stubborn pursuit of my highest good, he says, "Commit everything you do to the LORD. Trust him, and he will help you. . . . Be still in the presence of the LORD, and wait patiently for him to act" (Ps. 37:5, 7 NLT).

In addition to teaching me about his sweet consolations, waiting tests my faith. The truth is, I have no idea how strong my faith is until it's tested. When it is, I am assured it exists; and, in most cases, I am assured I need more faith than I have. But faith is a gift; I can't drum it up or talk myself into it. In my distress I must ask that my faith be increased. Were it not for my need, were it not for the wait, I wouldn't realize I need a faith fix more than a quick fix.

Though most of us want to avoid the pencil arrows that assail us, God, in his sovereign, wise, and stubborn love for us, refuses to rush in and do something that might temporarily relieve our panic . . . but leave us in much worse shape than we already are. Only God has the big picture of who we are becoming and what it will take to make us into his image. During our waiting, he carefully and meticulously performs the heart surgery we need. He knows just when and how to remove that which pierces us so deeply, and he does it without us bleeding to death in spite of what we fear.

Charles H. Spurgeon said: "I willingly bear witness to the fact that I owe more to my Lord's fire, hammer, and file than to anything else in his workshop. Sometimes I wonder if I have ever learned anything except at the end of God's rod. When my classroom is darkest, I see best."

Me too.

Trust that whatever action God is taking—or not taking—in your life right now is for your highest good. God knows what's he's doing.

Please Pass the Sandal

A year ago I experienced the most spirit-feeding, soul-
enhancing trip of my life. Together with my son, Jeff,
his wife, Carla, and my friend Pat, we joined several hundred others for pastor and radio host Chuck Swindoll's
tour through Israel.

Quite frankly, I did not anticipate the trip with much
excitement. I asked myself why I was going: Why spend
time and money on something for which I seemed to feel
so little enthusiasm? I would answer those ponderings
with guilt-laced thoughts like, *Marilyn, as a believer in
Christ and student of the Bible, you need to see the places
Jesus saw and the sites to which he referred. It will broaden
your borders and deepen your understandings.* With that bit
of moralizing I would try to dismiss the preferences that
sent me into reveries of the gentle, sunflower-splashed
hills of Tuscany with its luscious food and warmhearted
people. Why wasn't I going there instead, defying death
in a rented Fiat instead of nausea in a crowded tour bus?

At that point the most compelling aspect of the trip to
the Holy Land was the opportunity to spend two weeks
in the company of my son, Jeff, who, in my humble opinion, is the most engagingly fun and gifted young man on
the face of the earth!

In spite of my less-than-positive sentiments about the
trip, within hours of our arrival in Tel Aviv my entire
interior landscape began to change. It was not just that

our accommodations, food, and travel companions proved to be fantastic; there was an ever-increasing sense of God-was-here, God-continues-to-be-here, God-will-always-be-here. I'm not suggesting that I have to scout around to find God at home in Palm Desert, California, but there was an almost-palpable presence as we meandered from one biblically significant spot to another. The history of each was richly moving and spiritually rewarding.

As we all sat in the Roman theater in Caesarea, Chuck spoke briefly about covenant and how God has revealed himself as a covenant-making God. To those of us raised in the church, the word *covenant* is not unfamiliar, but I found myself latching onto it with new energy and interest. *Covenant* means "to chain together." It was the highest form of commitment two individuals could share. To covenant with someone was far more serious and binding than to promise.

My imagination was also sparked as I recalled several of the rituals used by people to enter into a covenant. A sword might be passed, signifying that the two would be united as one against the enemy. Or (and I hate this one) they might cut an animal in two and pass between its halves, the symbolism being that as each half, though separated, was still one animal, so the two covenant partners would become as one individual. Far more appealing to me was the ritual of two people passing a sandal between themselves, an action that symbolized they would travel any distance to be at each other's side.

What an incredible covenant God initiated with his creation, I thought, as we walked the huge Roman paving stones back to Bus 33. The God of Abraham, Isaac, and Jacob made a covenant with them and their many descendants who followed, saying: "I will live among you. . . . I will walk among you; I will be your God, and you will be my people" (Lev. 26:11–12 NLT).

And what an equally incredible, blatant disregard his people exhibited toward honoring that covenant! When warned by God about this through Jeremiah the prophet, the Israelites' response was "Don't waste your breath. We will continue to live as we want to, following our own evil desires" (Jer. 18:12 NLT). How could they! How could they refuse the covenant of an as-one relationship with the God of the universe? How stupid! And yet God kept hanging in there with them. Why would he even want to be "as-one" with those fickle people? How, after centuries of their nose-thumbing disobedience, could he say, "I will forgive their wickedness and will remember their sins no more" (Jer. 31:34)?

Well, I thought, as our tour bus headed out, *covenant or no covenant, I'd have bailed on that bunch. After all, they bailed first.*

Near our tour's conclusion we gathered in the tranquillity and beauty of the grounds at the Garden Tomb, located outside the walls of Jerusalem, a place many believe to be the site of the crucifixion and resurrection of Jesus. The lush garden of flowers and low-hanging trees was in stark contrast to the cacophony of sounds bombarding us from every direction: honking horns, bazaar owners yelling descriptions of their wares, grinding transmissions of hundreds of tour buses, as well as the Muslim muezzin calling his people to noontime prayer. Amazingly, in spite of the din beyond the garden walls, divine peace settled over our scene as Chuck led us into the "Remembrance of Me" service. *God was there.*

Aware of his presence and still munching on the word *covenant,* I realized in a fresh way that day that God's covenant with Israel was preparation for the coming of

God himself, in the person of his Son, to fulfill all his promises. With the failure of the Israelites to keep his covenant, God showed them the need for a new covenant that would bestow the power to obey.

The power to obey ... isn't that what we all need? It wasn't just the Israelites who blew it repeatedly and had to be jerk-chained back into line; it's every human being who's ever lived. We lack the power to obey. God knew his standard was humanly impossible, so he made sure we all knew that and then made a new covenant — one that provided for us a perfect person (Jesus) who, through his death on the cross, paid the price for our imperfection (sin). When I enter into that covenant relationship with Christ, I am washed with grace and welcomed as one of his people. My imperfection is forgiven, and God forgets it.

Grasping all this and incorporating it consistently will always be a challenge to me, even though Scripture repeatedly tells me I can do nothing in and of myself that will eliminate my bent toward disobedience. Nothing in and of myself will give me the power to obey other than his empowerment.

If I truly believe in the terms of the new covenant, I will recognize that it is the Holy Spirit of God, living in me, who produces that behavior for which I long, but, paradoxically, sometimes fight against. As Paul says, "I realize that I don't have what it takes. I can will it, but I can't *do* it. I decide to do good, but I don't *really* do it. I decide not to do bad, but then I do it anyway. My decisions, such as they are, don't result in actions" (Rom. 7:18–20 MSG). The answer to those struggles lies in accepting the terms of the new covenant: Jesus himself living within me, producing that which I can't.

What is behind that huge relief effort is God's love, a stubborn love that will not let me go, a love so tenacious, so gracious, so unfathomable, that he willingly made a new covenant with me at the highest price. That covenant is designed to assure me that in spite of poor performance, I am his and he is mine.

My guess is that we all need encouragement to relax in the grace of the new covenant and—ah, yes—to receive the sandal as it is passed.

O mad lover! It was
not enough for you to take
on our humanity; you had
to die for us as well.

CATHERINE OF SIENA

Death Threat in Aisle 17

Yesterday I was putting what I thought were the finishing touches on my grandchildren's Easter baskets. Standing back for a moment and eyeballing my handiwork, I realized that something was aesthetically "off." I couldn't quite figure out what it was. Then it dawned on me: the baskets needed that green grasslike stuff to cradle the little chocolate eggs and marshmallow bunnies. I well remembered the annoyance of that green stuff getting stuck in the carpet and nestling between the couch cushions to be discovered months later. As a young mother I lacked the patience for the untimely surfacing of Easter grass; now, as a grandmother, I eagerly went out to buy some.

My, how times have changed! There was no Easter grass as I remembered it. Instead, what was on the shelves was something called "Bunny Batts Funfil." It claims to be a "nontoxic, colorfast, no-mess, and no-loose-strands, flame-retardant" wonder for everything from Easter baskets to tree and plant bedding. Pleased with its color variety and soft feel, I bought a couple of bags. After all, I reasoned, I may decide to spruce up the look of my patio plants with a touch of lavender, pink, yellow, and emerald.

Having accomplished my task, I headed for the checkout counter, meandering through the aisles filled with everything from toilet plungers, car wax, slug bait, and orange juice to a variety of tweezers guaranteed to rid the body of visible nose hair, ear hair, and "unsightly knuckle hair." Mercy! Exiting the aisle devoted to eliminating the embarrassment of incontinence, I shifted my attention to a darling little toddler who was sitting in the front of his mom's shopping cart. His chubby little fists were full of multicolored M&Ms, which he was stuffing into his mouth with obvious pleasure.

The minute he saw me, however, his expression changed. He was apparently offended by the fact that I had grinned at him and winked. With a look of unmistakable hostility, he took a minute to size me up, and then awkwardly flung his fistful of M&Ms in my direction.

Pretending to be afraid, I ducked behind the Attends display, waited a second, and then peeked out at him. His expression had not changed or his aim improved. Once again he attempted to pelt me with M&Ms. Realizing that my playful spirit did nothing but add to his antagonism, I decided to escape down a side aisle before the whole bag of candy was hurled at me.

Amazingly enough, this little fellow's mother was totally unaware of the drama unfolding only a few feet from her. She appeared to be so fully engrossed in the claims of a miracle-working tooth whitener that she completely missed the skirmishes of her tiny warrior.

I have smiled repeatedly over this incident since its occurrence nearly twenty-four hours ago. The experience intrigues me not just because of the ferocity of the baby battler, whom I actually found appealing, but also because it nudges me into deeper contemplation. For example, other than the possibility that my grin and wink is sufficiently unattractive as to produce acts of violence, I was innocent. I did not deserve the treatment I was getting. Why should my warm-hearted intentions be so furiously rebuffed?

The reason those questions stay with me is that they are not unfamiliar. There have been times when people (other than toddlers) have seemingly misunderstood my motives and reacted negatively. I have left the experience thinking, *What was that all about? I didn't deserve that.* In almost all cases the problem was one of miscommunication and was ultimately solved with a clarifying conversation.

But I have to admit that a few of my experiences with God have fallen into the category of *What did I do to deserve this? What are you doing? Do you care?* Or worse, *Do you even know what's going on down here?!* Perhaps you have asked the same questions from time to time. When our lives are unexpectedly interrupted with tension, pain, or loss, our tendency is to cast about trying to figure it all out — and thereby hopefully change the outcome of events. At least that's my tendency.

I was in one of those major questioning modes a few months ago as I struggled to grasp the enormity of the health issues that threatened to keep me from fulfilling my speaking and writing obligations for months into the future. If I had been totally honest with God, I'd have confessed to him my fear that my needs might have gotten lost somewhere in the global hubbub. I felt neglected. I was startled, then, to read in my Bible one particularly vulnerable morning:

> Why do you say, O Jacob, and complain, O Israel, "My way is hidden from the LORD; my cause is disregarded by my God"?

> ISAIAH 40:27

Frankly, I felt almost embarrassed. My whiny fear that God may have overlooked my needs was addressed in bold print right there in his Word. Not only did he acknowledge my struggle, but he also went on in the next verse to remind me that "his understanding no one can fathom." I'll never be able to figure out God's ways, and certainly it is not within my power to change the events of my life, or their outcome, if God himself has set those events in motion.

But he didn't leave me with my feelings of shame and foolishness. God's not like that. Rather, he pronounced a lavish promise that soothed my soul to the core:

> He gives strength to the weary
> and increases the power of the weak.
> Even youths grow tired and weary,
> and young men stumble and fall;
> but those who hope in the LORD
> will renew their strength.
> They will soar on wings like eagles;
> they will run and not grow weary,
> they will walk and not be faint.
>
> ISAIAH 40:29–31

I took that promise very personally: "He gives strength to weary Marilyn and increases her power when she is weak. She *will* mount up with wings like an eagle." Little did I know as my spirit was encouraged that morning that God would soon literally supply physical strength and unexpected power for my body. Praise his name!

I know my battles aren't over. I know yours aren't either. But isn't it a comfort to know that our God's love is never miserly, never punishing of our secret, doubt-plagued thoughts? He will never pelt us in anger. He will never leave us, even when we whine and throw tantrums in our frustration over what we don't like or don't understand. After all, he knows we're just candy-tossing toddlers at heart.

*As a father has compassion on his children, so the
LORD has compassion on those who fear him; for he
knows how we are formed, he remembers that we
are dust.*

PSALM 103:13–14

Riding on the Rims

The papers described her as the woman who shouted "Praise God, yeah!" as she streaked past the finish line. She was also named the most endearing image from the 104th Boston marathon as she bellowed the National Anthem with a victory wreath on her head, a grin on her face, and radiant delight in her heart. This winner dynamo is Jean Driscoll, the first person ever to win the Boston marathon eight times.

Behind that impressive fact, however, is an inspiring and compelling story. Jean was born with spina bifida. As a child she walked with the aid of crutches, but at age fifteen she was forced to start using a wheelchair. What she had feared would be limiting instead opened up a new world to her. She found that in a wheelchair she could finally play sports: soccer, football, water skiing, basketball, and then racing. In her chair, she can cover 26.2 miles in one hour and thirty-four minutes. In case you need a comparison to grasp that statistic, she is thirty-two minutes faster than the men's able-bodied marathon world record.

I met Jean for the first time several years ago when she wheeled up to my book table in Cincinnati at the conclusion of a Women of Faith conference. I had told the story there of our baby, Joanie, who had been born with spina bifida and died when she was fifteen days old. Jean was touched by my experience and felt God nudge her to introduce herself to me. At the time I had no idea she was a record-breaking, world-renowned athlete; I knew simply that she was in a wheelchair and that, as she told me, she too had been born with spina bifida. I found myself deeply touched by this obviously well-educated, bright, vivacious young woman who just happened to be the same age as Joanie would have been.

In addition to the almost instant attachment I felt toward Jean, I also felt a definite "Godness" in our meeting. He had something in mind far greater than just that sweet encounter. We have stayed in touch through periodic phone calls and letters. She never fails to inspire me or move my spirit at a deep level.

God has used her in an especially significant way in the past few months in regard to my own physical restrictions. Jean shared with me her race defeat in 1997 when her chair caught on the MBTA trolley tracks, throwing her timing off completely. Then she lost another competition in a race so close the winner had to be determined by replaying the videotape. Utterly discouraged, she went six weeks without training, even contemplating retirement from the sport. I too had wondered if I had "lost the race." Should I just retire, thus freeing Women of Faith to find a replacement speaker?

On the morning of March 7, 2000, the phone rang. It was a jubilant Jean Driscoll calling from Los Angeles to tell me she had just won the L.A. marathon! She was hesitant to call because she knew I was struggling for enough stamina just to walk to my mailbox, and she didn't want to "bother me." I had known she was training for L.A., that she still wasn't sure what God wanted to do with her racing career, and that if she won, it was definitely God's deal. I was thrilled to hear from her and asked for details about the latest victory.

She told me that toward the end of the race, with her opponents well behind her, the carbon fiber wheels on her racing chair gave out; she was reduced to riding on the rims. Determined not to quit or be defeated, she rounded a corner where an unexpected pit crew tore over to her chair, replaced the tires in seconds, and sent her on her way . . . a way that produced a first-place victory.

While I listened to her account I had the strongest sense that God was saying to me: "Listen carefully to this, Marilyn. You, at this moment, are riding on the rims. Trust me for ultimate victory—the race is not over."

I must admit that when I hung up the phone I accused myself of being in la-la land, that my personal identification with Jean's victory probably had more to do with motherly instincts toward her than God's word to me. Nevertheless, I couldn't seem to quiet the message that urged me on in a race that God said was not over.

Ten days later, trusting his prompting, I flew to San Jose, California, where I spoke at my first conference of the year. (Three others had already taken place without me.) While God certainly cannot be reduced to a "pit crew," I was deeply aware of him rushing to my aid and then sending me on my way that weekend. In fact, he continues to do just that for me. He makes it possible to do what I do and then cheers me on.

And yet I have to admit that I am constantly challenged by his promise that he "is able to do immeasurably more than all we ask or imagine, according to his power that is at work within us" (Eph. 3:20). Why in the world I limit the power or provision of the God of the universe is beyond me. I'm embarrassed by my lack of faith in his loving abundance. He states over and over in his Word that "there is no God like me," and I believe that to be true. My problem is receiving and incorporating into my straggling life all that he is and all that he promises to be in my needy state.

This morning I was inspired and even amused as I read a classic piece written by Hannah Whitall Smith. She referenced the passage from 2 Kings 6:17 where God gave Elisha "chariots of fire" to be used in battle, assuring him of victory. According to that passage, not everyone could see the chariots—only those whose eyes God opened. Smith writes:

> Lord, open our eyes so we may see God's chariots of fire. God's chariots are waiting to transport us to places of victory. Once our eyes are opened by God, we will see all the events of our lives, whether great or small, joyful or sad, as a chariot for our souls. Everything that comes to us becomes a chariot the moment we treat it as such.

After reading this I thought, *Well, Marilyn, honey . . . why should you be riding on the rims when you could be streaking about in a chariot of fire?* I've always loved a flashy, fast mode of transportation, and as long as God keeps my eyes open to his lavishly loving provision, I've got one!

Wanna race?

The Hair Prayer

Imagine this: Even as I write these words, there is a flotilla of "Rugrats" doll heads floating toward Alaska. (How about that for a piece of information I can toss out during a conversational lull?) A month ago, tens of thousands of Tommy Pickles doll heads designed for a Mattel's animated TV show managed to fall overboard from the ship that carried them toward their destination. They are now making their current-propelled way to various destinations in the world. Two heads have already been found in Oregon, one in Washington, and thirteen in British Columbia's Queen Charlotte Islands. A scientist who was put on "doll alert" and tracks ocean currents says a big patch of heads is expected to bump onto the shores of Alaska anytime.

Apparently each head is about the size of a coconut without a husk. Can you imagine anything more unnerving than strolling along a shoreline somewhere, thinking your usual deep, contemplative thoughts, when suddenly a Pickle head emerges from the water's edge, rolls awkwardly toward your sandy sneakers, and then stares woodenly up at you? *Am I really seeing this?* you might wonder. *Maybe I really did flunk that Rorschach test.* At that point of self-doubt it would be a comfort if a few thousand more heads surfaced so that at least you could say with confidence, "Yes, I really am seeing this!" Of course, the how and why of the strange experience would present a new array of challenges.

Much as I'd love it, nothing as outlandishly quirky as a marooned Pickle head has ever come into my line of vision. But there have been many times when I've second-guessed what I saw and speculated about my ability to "get the picture" accurately.

My most recent experience with this was three and a half weeks ago. I was talking to God about something that rather embarrassed me even to bring up but that was a sufficiently strong concern for me to say, "Okay, I'm going to pray about this even though I think the subject indicates I am a shallow woman whose priorities need realignment." Let me give you a little background on what prompted my prayer.

One of my physical responses to the poison still working its way out of my system has been hair loss. All my life I have been basically hair and teeth — no face, just hair and teeth. But I was fast becoming just teeth. Now, in the grand scheme of recovery I felt the hair concern was minor, but when I brought it up to God he didn't indicate that it was minor at all. In fact, I was stunned by the divine response I sensed clearly in my spirit.

The oft-repeated Old Testament phrase stated by God to his people and prophets is, ". . .that you might know that I am God." In other words, God would do something for his people that only God could do: part the Red Sea; defeat the giant Goliath through the boy David; raise up a field of bones to life; produce torrential rains from a previously cloudless sky to overwhelm the worshippers of the idol Baal, etc. God would conclude these various demonstrations of his miraculous power by explaining, ". . . that you might know that I am God." When I prayed my hair prayer, there was the immediate inner assurance that hair would indeed come, for the purpose of Marilyn "knowing" that God is God.

I must add that there was another little desire I threw out to God during the hair prayer. I asked God if hair growth could occur in time for our yearly Women of Faith photo shoot, scheduled for only three weeks hence. Quite frankly, I thought I was really pushing it, but asked anyway.

Of course, the enemy of our souls loves to "undo" our faith in God's promises to us, so it wasn't long before I was questioning what God actually meant when he assured me: yes, it was okay for me to pray for hair and, yes, he was going to provide it. I began not only to second-guess the divine invitation to bring my every care to him (Ps. 55:22), but also to doubt the assurance that he was going to give me exactly what I'd asked for. After all, children and adults are dying of cancer, people are confined to wheelchairs, strokes reduce once-vigorous people to needy dependency, refugees displaced and traumatized by ethnic cleansing desperately struggle just to survive . . . and I have the nerve to ask God for mere hair in the midst of such crushing human affliction? In short, I quickly condemned myself as well as my prayer as inexcusably vain and utterly inappropriate.

However, in spite of my embarrassed inner protests, the contrasting message "that you may know that I am God" continued to reverberate in my spirit.

As the days passed I noticed that the sink was increasingly clear of the little hair nests that normally nestled in the drain following every shampoo. One morning I peered into the mirror and tentatively asked out loud, "Am I seeing what I think I'm seeing?" Dozens and dozens of wiry little hair sprouts were poking out all over my pink scalp. Surely not . . . surely yes. Incredible! How can that be? Why would God . . . you mean he *really?*

I flew to the photo shoot last week with my wildly sprouting and totally unmanageable new hair. The recent growth was undeniable. So was God's fulfilled promise. And so is my gratitude. My dear friends — Luci, Patsy, Thelma, Barbara, and Sheila — listened eagerly as I told them about the hair prayer and God's response. Not one of them seemed to think I'd careened off my spiritual trolley tracks, but instead entered completely into my blessing. They also voiced a strong "no" to the wig I had purchased when I feared God might need a backup plan for the photo shoot. They all said my own new hair was far better. (I could swear I heard God chuckle over that.)

I cannot even begin to understand or explain the divine "why" of this hair experience. My husband died at age fifty-two of cancer; our baby died when she was two weeks old; scores of people prayed, but God did not choose to do what I longed for. Why not? Does he love me more now than he did then? No. God simply does what he does because he's God. I'll never figure him out. The hair prayer experience just reminded me again: "'My thoughts are completely different from yours,' says the LORD. 'And my ways are far beyond anything you could imagine. For just as the heavens are higher than the earth, so are my ways higher than your ways and my thoughts higher than your thoughts'" (Isa. 55:8–9 NLT).

Here's the only thing I do know about the hair deal: The hair is merely something visible that God is using tangibly to assure me of his divine power, his sovereign design to raise me up again in spite of how I feel or even look, and the outlandish lengths to which he'll go to reassure me of his love and power. Why he goes to all that trouble is beyond me, but he states clearly: "I am God and there is no other; I am God, and there is none like me. I make known the end from the beginning, from ancient times, what is still to come. I say: My purpose will stand, and I will do all that I please" (Isa. 46:9–10).

When God says his purpose will stand and that he does what he pleases, my part in it all is to sit back humbly, receive whatever it is he plans for me, and *believe* in what I see. Right now his divine touch is impossible not to see . . . it's sprigging up all over my head! Why? ". . . that you might know, Marilyn . . . that you might know."

Even to your old age and gray hairs I am he, I am he who will sustain you. I have made you and I will carry you; I will sustain you and I will rescue you.

ISAIAH 46:4

The Ultimate Power Source

Yesterday, in the midst of one of my mindless thinks, I startled myself with a thought. Because my mind had been formless and void, it was a notable moment. Interestingly enough the thought was not new, but it came with such intensity it had the feel of new. It was this: *Greater power is available to all God's people.*

Well . . . since I am one of God's people, I had to personalize that thought. I certainly recognized my frequent sense of powerlessness, so the prospect of greater power was compelling. If more power is available, how do I get it?

The metaphor that came to me was that of an electrical outlet. When I need power for anything (my wild boar meat strainer or vegetable puree-mash mixer) I plug in. Simple. So am I not "plugged in" to God's power? After all, I'm a Christian . . . I study my Bible . . . I pray. Do I need bigger plugs? What am I missing?

Let me seemingly go down a rabbit trail and tell you an experience I had with my golf cart. To begin with, I adore my golf cart. My schedule keeps me off the golf course (which ensures the physical well-being of all within range of my unpredictably wild and erratic shots), but the cart is my mode of transportation around the condominium complex in which I live. My neighbors and I toodle to each other's homes via our respective golf carts . . . never a car.

One balmy late afternoon I called my neighbor Luci and asked her to join me in my cart for a quick beyond-our-gates trip to the pharmacy.

"Is your cart street-legal, Marilyn? Are you supposed to drive it on public roads?"

"No . . . but we aren't going far, and we'll take the back streets."

Quickly convinced, Luci and I took off to pick up my hormones.

On the ride home I felt fully confident that my little cart was destined for every public thoroughfare in America. I breathed in the scent of citrus blossoms, reveled in my radio's reception of Vivaldi's *Four Seasons,* and said to Luci, "In the words of some beer commercial, it doesn't get any better than this."

As she was about to agree, my cart did an unprecedented cough, and belch, skipped two heartbeats . . . and died. Not only did my cart die dead away, we were in the middle of a fairly busy intersection. With a squealing of brakes, several cars went careening off left and right in an attempt to avoid rear-ending us. As we breathlessly pushed her (my cart . . . I call her a "her" . . . actually, her name is Celeste) onto the sidewalk, I kept telling Luci, "She can't have a dead battery! Look, the lights are on, and the radio's still doing Vivaldi. Not only that, she was plugged into the power charger for several hours this morning; she's been fully juiced!"

"Juice or no juice, Marilyn, how do you expect to get this fully charged baby home?"

Grimly talking our way through as many unworkable plans as we could think of, I got the brilliant idea of calling AAA for emergency roadside assistance. After all, I was in a disabled vehicle by the side of the road. I'd been a club member for over thirty years and hardly ever called them. It was the perfect time!

By now it was completely dark. Were it not for the intersection streetlights I'd never have been able to make out the emergency phone number on the back of my AAA card. Successfully punching in the number on Luci's cell phone, I tried to explain my predicament to the very, very young male who received my call. He commiserated with me about my breakdown, took my street location, and then asked for a description of my vehicle.

"Well . . . my vehicle is small . . . kind of convertible-like. It's turquoise with a tan top. And my name, Marilyn, is written in script letters on the left-hand side." After a long pause, the very, very young voice asked, "Ma'am . . . are you describing a car?"

"Uh, no . . . I'm describing my disabled vehicle."

With absolutely no effort at self-control, he began to laugh and said it sounded as if I was describing a golf cart. When I owned up to that fact, he laughed even harder and told me that AAA did not "assist" golf carts.

"Well, how about a golf cart owner and her friend who are both very, very old and sitting on a sidewalk in the dark, unprotected in a bad neighborhood, with no hope of assistance or even defense should someone decide to prey on the elderly?" (Actually, it was not a bad neighborhood, but we were old, and I knew Celeste was dangerously appealing.)

That plea seemed to spark a helpful spirit in the boy. He told me he'd give our location to a tow-truck company who would haul us home, but it would be at my expense. Forty-five minutes later, an enormous flatbed truck pulled up. After assuring the driver that my cart was indeed the vehicle to be hauled, Celeste was hoisted up with huge cable chains and placed in the middle of the truck, where she settled conspicuously with room for at least two Winnebagos on either side of her. Luci and I heaved our way up into the truck cab, which was at least thirty-one feet higher than the street surface, and with much commotion, including flashing lights, we made our way to my quiet, unsuspecting neighborhood, where Celeste deftly slid down the ramp into my garage.

The next morning the "cart doctor" made a house call. I learned that in spite of Celeste being fully charged from my conscientious "plug in," her battery wires had short-circuited, which produced a wire meltdown.

So, you must be wondering, *what in the world is this woman's point? What does all this have to do with that now-faraway thought during her mindless think?* Here's how it connects for me; see if it does for you as well.

The realization that God intends for each of us greater power than we are currently experiencing is tremendously encouraging. From his original intentionality, from before the foundation of the world, God intended for us to be power-based. That is, *Power*-based. Though we may be "plugged in" as it relates to salvation, prayer, and Bible study, sometimes we nevertheless short-circuit, lose power, and go dead in the middle of life's intersections. We don't lose our salvation; we don't lose his love. But we lose power.

So, how do we get it back? More important, how do we hang onto it and not lose it in the first place? The answer lies in the use of the name Jesus. His name is the ultimate power source. The apostle Paul said in his letter to the Christians at Philippi: "God highly exalted Him, and bestowed on Him the name which is above every name, so that at the name of Jesus every knee will bow ... every tongue will confess that Jesus Christ is Lord" (Phil. 2:9–11 NASB).

Scripture reminds us repeatedly of the power in that holy name and urges us to use it for our every need.

Shortly before Jesus left the earth, he specifically advised his disciples on the use of his name, saying, "Until now you have asked for nothing in My name; ask, and you will receive, so that your joy may be made full" (John 16:24 NASB). Jesus pointed out to his followers that using his name in prayer was new, but from that moment on he intended that they would have constant access to a new power source . . . his name.

In my life's current intersection, I've realized anew that though I remain plugged in simply because my faithful God won't disconnect from me, my sense of powerlessness that comes and goes may lie simply in my forgetting or neglecting to use the Name. I may be too overwhelmed, tired, or sick even to present my needs to God. When that happens I can simply say the Name: Jesus . . . Jesus . . . Jesus. When there are no words, when there is no strength, there is always his Name.

There is no greater Power source, my friend. God's boundless love provides it; his intent is that we use it.

My hope is built on nothing less
Than Jesus' blood and righteousness;
I dare not trust the sweetest frame,
But wholly lean on Jesus' name.

EDWARD MOTE

Women of Faith partners with various Christian
organizations, including Zondervan,
Campus Crusade for Christ International,
Crossings Book Club, Integrity Music,
International Bible Society,
Partnerships, Inc., and World Vision
to provide spiritual resources for women.

For more information about Women of Faith
or to register for one of our nationwide conferences,
call 1-800-49-FAITH.

www.women-of-faith.com

Coming Soon from Women of Faith℠

The Women of Faith Daily Devotional

Available January 2002

366 Devotions

In their own inimitable fashion, the six Women of Faith—Patsy Clairmont, Barbara Johnson, Marilyn Meberg, Luci Swindoll, Sheila Walsh, and Thelma Wells—show what it's like to live as a woman of faith. Day by day, in 366 devotions, they touch on and illumine twelve foundational aspects of faith:

January—Hope	July—Freedom
February—Prayer	August—Humor
March—Friendship	September—Vitality
April—Wonder	October—Trust
May—Grace	November—Gratitude
June—Joy	December—Peace

Drawing from their varied life experiences, both painful and delightful, the six authors reveal their triumphs and joys with humor, love, and grace to enrich all their readers with their hard-won wisdom, infused by the light of Scripture.

Hardcover 0-310-24069-7   Burgandy Bonded Leather 0-310-24150-2

Also Available:
NIV Woman of Faith Study Bible
Hardcover 0-310-91883-9
Softcover 0-310-91884-7
Violet Bonded Leather 0-310-91885-5

Women of Faith Devotionals

Joy Breaks
Hardcover 0-310-21345-2

We Brake for Joy!
Hardcover 0-310-22042-4
Audio Pages® Abridged Cassettes 0-
310-22434-9

OverJoyed!
Hardcover 0-310-22653-8
Audio Pages® Abridged Cassettes
0-310-22760-7

Extravagant Grace
Hardcover 0-310-23125-6
Audio Pages® Abridged
Cassettes 0-310-23126-4

Resources for Women of Faith℠

BOOKS/AUDIO

The Joyful Journey	Hardcover	0-310-21344-4
	Softcover	0-310-22155-2
	Audio Pages® Abridged Cassettes	0-310-21454-8
	Daybreak	0-310-97282-5
Bring Back the Joy	Hardcover	0-310-22023-8
	Softcover	0-310-22915-4
	Audio Pages® Abridged Cassettes	0-310-22222-2
Outrageous Joy	Hardcover	0-310-22648-1
	Audio Pages® Abridged Cassettes	0-310-22660-0

WOMEN OF FAITH BIBLE STUDY SERIES

Celebrating Friendship	0-310-21338-X
Discovering Your Spiritual Gifts	0-310-21340-1
Embracing Forgiveness	0-310-21341-X
Experiencing God's Presence	0-310-21343-6
Finding Joy	0-310-21336-3
Growing in Prayer	0-310-21335-5
Knowing God's Will	0-310-21339-8
Strengthening Your Faith	0-310-21337-1

WOMEN OF FAITH WOMEN OF THE BIBLE STUDY SERIES

Deborah: Daring to Be Different for God	0-310-22662-7
Esther: Becoming a Woman God Can Use	0-310-22663-5
Hannah: Entrusting Your Dreams to God	0-310-22667-8
Mary: Choosing the Joy of Obedience	0-310-22664-3
Ruth: Trusting That God Will Provide for You	0-310-22665-1
Sarah: Facing Life's Uncertainties with a Faithful God	0-310-22666-X

WOMEN OF FAITH Zondervan*Groupware*™

Capture the Joy	Video Curriculum Kit	0-310-23096-9
	Leader's Guide	0-310-23101-9
	Participant's Guide	0-310-23099-3

*Inspirio's innovative and elegant gift books
capture the joy and encouragement that is an integral part
of the Women of Faith^{SM} movement.*

Joy for a Woman's Soul
Promises to Refresh Your Spirit
ISBN: 0-310-97717-7

Grace for a Woman's Soul
Reflections to Renew Your Spirit
ISBN: 0-310-97996-X

Simple Gifts
*Unwrapping the Special
Moments of Everyday Life*
ISBN: 0-310-97811-4

**Hope for a
Woman's Soul**
*Meditations to
Energize Your
Spirit*
ISBN: 0-310-98010-0

Padded Hardcover
4 x 7
208 pages

*Verses from the New International Version of
the Bible have been collected into these topically arranged volumes
to inspire Women of Faith^{SM} on their spiritual journey.*

Prayers for a Woman of Faith^{SM}
ISBN: 0-310-97336-8

**Words of Wisdom
for a Woman of Faith^{SM}**
ISBN: 0-310-97390-2

**Promises of Joy
for a Woman of Faith^{SM}**
ISBN: 0-310-97389-9

**Words of Wisdom
for a Woman of Faith^{SM}**
ISBN: 0-310-97735-5

**Psalms and Proverbs
for a Woman of Faith^{SM}**
ISBN: 0-310-98092-5

**Promises of Love
for a Woman of Faith^{SM}**
ISBN: 0-310-98249-9

Hardcover
5-1/4 x 5-1/4
128 pages

We want to hear from you. Please send your comments about this book to us in care of the address below. Thank you.

GRAND RAPIDS, MICHIGAN 49530

www.zondervan.com